P9-ECT-910

DATE DUE

NOV 1 2 1979		
MAR 2 5 1996		
GAYLORD 334		PRINTED IN U. S. A.

Sparrow on the House Top

Sparrow on the House Top

by Ruth Hunt

Reaching beyond loneliness
to true peace and joy

/6062

Fleming H. Revell Company
Old Tappan, New Jersey

Scripture quotations in this volume are based on the King James Version of the Bible

Poem from "THE CLIFF'S EDGE: SONGS OF A PSYCHOTIC" by Eithne Tabor, Copyright, 1950, Sheed and Ward, Inc., New York.

Library of Congress Cataloging in Publication Data

Hunt, Ruth.
     Sparrow on the house top.

     1. Bible—Biography. 2. Loneliness. I. Title.
BS571.H793   242'.4   76–18182
ISBN 0–8007–0814–8

TO
David

Contents

And is
There anyone at all?
I am knocking at the oaken door . . .
And will it open
Never now no more?
I am calling, calling to you—
Don't you hear?
And is there anyone
Near?
And does this empty silence have to be?
And is there no one there at all
To answer me?

I do not know the road—
I fear to fall
And is there anyone
At all?

From *The Cliff's Edge: Songs of a Psychotic.*

1

This Empty Silence

On an overpass balustrade high above a gleaming stretch of the Hollywood Freeway, carrying on its graceful sweep the minutiae of thousands upon thousands of steel-encapsulated human beings, perches the figure of a woman. Just an instant it pauses—poised against the smog-tinged blue of morning sky —then plunges to the pavement below.

In a nearby prosperous suburban community, a college student—last year the cheerleader of his graduating high-school class—popular, handsome, sure to succeed—hangs himself in despair over the unbearable anonymity he feels in the impersonal milieu of a teeming city campus.

In one of our large and better-run children's homes, over-crowded of course, as all such institutions are, a child of seven retreats into a fantasy world where a clutched length of blanket becomes a mother's apron—ever-present, comforting, eternally transformed into a thing of warmth and intimacy.

Written in the diary of an elderly inner-city pensioner is found the entry, "Nobody came today," penned with uniform regularity day after day—year after year—until death finally ends the bleak recital.

What these acts—two of them desperate and final—meant in terms of human misery, all of us can identify with in some degree. Loneliness, the universal disease that has been termed by Dr. Paul Tournier, the eminent Swiss psychiatrist, "The most devastating malady of our age," has touched us all. But the disturbing thing—horrifying for its victims and damning for the rest of us—is that all of the incidents cited above happened in places or circumstances far from being solitary.

In the sure knowledge that not one of the thousands of human beings stretching back to an infinity of asphalt miles cares about her, Jane Doe jumps. Traffic stops, the LAPD mobilizes its efficient emergency forces, hundreds of passing motorists crane their necks in horrified fascination. A small part of a great metropolis has been brought to a standstill and unwillingly participates in a wake of sorts for the nonentity that was Jane Doe. A voice has spoken—just as surely as if it had been audible to each of the spectators:

"Look at me. You don't know my pain, but now, at last, you must share this much of my agony."

And the pathos of that terrible thud does make an impact— for a moment at least.

The dictionary defines *loneliness* as the state of being isolated, unaccompanied, solitary. Certainly in none of these cases was this *physically* true. It is the great irony of our time that along with our desperate effort to stem the alarming population explosion which threatens to literally elbow us off the earth, the seemingly incurable malady of which Dr. Tournier speaks is infecting ever-greater segments of that increasing population. Existing in close proximity to other people does not insure a feeling of relatedness. James Thomson's poem "William Blake" expresses it poignantly.

> He came to the desert of London town,
>   Gray miles long;
> He wandered up and he wandered down
>   Singing a quiet song.

He came to the desert of London town,
  Mirk miles broad;
He wandered up and he wandered down,
  Ever alone with God.

There were thousands and thousands of human kind
  In this desert of brick and stone:
But some were deaf and some were blind,
  And he was there alone.

At length the good hour came; he died
  As he had lived, alone:
He was not missed from the desert wide,
  Perhaps he was found at the Throne.

Indeed, existence within a mass of people often accentuates the feeling of loneliness. We know that despite the proximity, no relationship exists—and we resent this as human beings. There may be no more devastating experience for a country-bred person than to come with high hopes to the city—either job- or college-bound—and to find himself in an unresponsive dorm or office full of people. At home solitude had been expected, but here—the excitement, the activity, the vitality of the dreamed-of metropolis—and none of it touches him.

Examples are without number. The young couple immigrates to America from England. They've been told how free and easy and disarmingly open the Yankees are, and they're not disappointed—at first. Everyone has a glib and ready greeting. "From England? How charming. You must meet my aunt. She's from London. Any children? How lovely. Ours are the same age. They would get along well. Where are you living? Great! That's near us. We *must* get together." It takes the newcomers a while to realize that the exchange was just that—an exchange of words carried on as part of a game in which each player stays on his side of an invisible line and tosses phrases back and forth. One never invades the other's territory. Neither do they meet the aunt, nor are the children given the opportunity to "get along well," nor do the couples ever "get together."

Of course the freeway becomes the ultimate symbol of impersonalization. That it can transform a mild-mannered human being into an uninhibited exhibitionist of bad manners all of us have experienced. Those others out there beyond the tinted glass have lost their reality. They've become part of a mass, and toward a "mass" one cannot feel a community of spirit, of sympathy, or compassion—or even of courtesy. The things that we mutter to ourselves or toss out the window of a moving automobile would never be dared face to face.

Then there is the aloneness of a large university dorm where one has no intimate friend with whom to share either joys or frustrations. Or it can be the crush of a subway car as one is bumped and shuffled about and made painfully aware that one is being physically jostled but not emotionally touched—when one perhaps very much needs just that. It can even mean the long walk down a church aisle to sit in a pew alone, wondering whether someone—a stranger—*anyone*—will stop to fill up some part of that long emptiness of polished wood.

It's the milling crowd of a busy airport with its hundreds of preoccupied people, greeting friends, taking leave, or perhaps just standing still, waiting behind the raised newspaper—each locked in his own world. The poet Rupert Brooke, embarking on a voyage from his native England, found the pain of friendless departure too great to bear. Seeing a lad lounging idly on the pier, he sent a message and a coin down to him with the request that he should watch for a gentleman such as he described at the rail, and when the ship passed out of the harbor he should *wave*. So much did he want his lonely departure to be shared by some other human being!

"It is not good that man should be alone." That wise maxim is built into the human spirit and it is just as true today as ever it was in the Garden. That America's social workers and psychologists recognize the malady of loneliness is abundantly clear. Psychiatric research and therapy is given an ever-more prominent place, especially as it relates to the increasing problems of an urbanization that thrusts people into closer and closer proximity to one another and at the same time depersonalizes and alienates. Even our classified ads attest to an awareness of the need and the attempts made to meet it. Hot Lines, Computerized Dating, Dial-a-Date, Dial-a-Prayer, and a myriad of other similar channels for meeting human needs are signs of our times.

That we Americans respond sympathetically to the needs of the world community is proverbial. We are known as a charitable nation, giving generously to humane causes. We are justly proud of being in the forefront in our support of the Red Cross, world famine relief, and most recently in our sympathetic reception of thousands of Vietnamese refugees and orphans. Collections for heart, cancer, muscular dystrophy, and birth defects research and cure are only a few among many channels of concerned giving.

But important as they may be, these are, after all, impersonal acts. The dollar so generously given by someone half a world away and added to other dollars similarly sent will buy the sack of beans that keeps a village alive, but it will not assuage the inner need which cries out for contact with someone who cares specifically and personally for *me*. And granted that a would-be suicide accepts the fact that the person on the other end of the Hot Line has a genuine interest in helping, but how personally involved is a disembodied voice connected by a system of wires and electronic devices? That fragile connection can be broken in a moment. Though there may be the most genuine love of Christ motivating the counselor on the other end, unless it makes solid and conscious contact with the one seeking help, the moment will be lost—literally a broken connection. And all those brittle and surface minglings which social convention demands of the civilized herd remain just that—a "mingling" and a rubbing of elbows, but never the relationship which in a certain degree makes of two human beings one spirit.

"Loneliness seems to be such a painful, frightening experience that people will do practically everything to avoid it." So said the well-known psychologist Frieda Fromm-Reichmann in her book *Psychoanalysis and Psychotherapy.* The first trauma an infant knows is to be left alone with strangers. The next is often to be shut up in a dark room. The fear of not only being without familiar human companionship but also of being cut off from visual relationship with one's environment becomes an abiding memory which often reaches into adulthood. Hell itself has been described as "a blackness of darkness forever." Its chief terror is one of total and eternal separation—the unrelatedness of one who was designed by his Maker not to exist alone.

The fear of loneliness has caused young men and women to marry unloved, to forget their moral standards, to change their personalities, to retreat to an imaginary world, and finally—in alarming numbers—to commit suicide. It will cause a battered child to fight the efforts of a kindly judge to separate it from its abusive mother. A teenager will accept a friend—any friend at all—in preference to no friend. No amount of criticism or raised-eyebrow questioning on his parents' part will wring from him the admission that this was the best he could find, that he knows this person is unworthy of his time and loyalty, but he *must* have a friend. Indeed there seems such an instinctive recoil from existing in a state of unrelatedness in this very impersonal world, that even the non-Christian must seriously wonder whether somewhere a very ideal and divine human relationship hasn't been lost and is evermore being sought.

All the symptoms of twentieth-century life bear out the above premises. From youth to old age man is involved in an identity crisis of gargantuan proportions. It can be traced in every stage of development. *Science Digest* ("The Biology of Loneliness, December, 1973) describes the work done at the Regional Primate Research Center at Wisconsin University, where Dr. William T. McKinney, Jr., separated a group of monkeys three to five months old from their mothers and observed the results. The immediate reaction was one of hyperactivity, closely related to the behavior of an autistic child. They were registering protest against maternal deprivation. This stage was replaced thirty-six to forty-eight hours later, however, by a deepening withdrawal state. The unpleasantly exhibited demand not having been met, the monkeys lapsed into an attitude of despair. When their brains were examined, a number of imbalances were found. The most significant of these was an increased amount of serotonin, an organic compound that acts as a sedative. It is known that large amounts of this excretion can cause schizophrenic symptoms. In other experiments, five-to-ten week-old mice separated from their mothers showed the same symptoms of depression and withdrawal. Even more significantly, on their return to communal living they quickly developed insufferably aggressive traits, becoming intense, nervous, and scrappy fighters. Brain examinations again showed biological change, with the discovery that they possessed fewer than the normal number of inhibitory nerve endings.

What these findings presage for the whole developing structure of our society would seem to be no less than a resounding disaster. When we stack up the demands voiced by the hundreds of delegates to the International Women's Year Congress in Mexico City beside the less militantly expressed plaints of countless unwanted and burdensome children, one readily sees where the advantage lies. That we have birth-control clinics and child-care centers being built as fast as steel and mortar can be laid—and at the same time are engaging in a losing race to establish Juvenile Detention Homes and Suicide Prevention Centers as fast as the need escalates—presents an anomaly that can escape few perceptive hearts. With women by the thousands abdicating their responsibilities as mothers in favor of more "fulfilling" involvements, we are left with a whole generation of children who know very well their lack of acceptance and approval. With an inborn sensitivity created to recognize and respond to love, they know that indeed they are a hindrance to so-called better things.

"Don't bother me!" How many times has this deadly order fallen like a shroud on a child's blooming and developing spirit. As surely as he will either raise a fist in his own defense or will shrink back to ward off a blow, that child will respond with alienating aggressive behavior or will retreat to an inner isolation where he feels safe from further hurt. Though the former is the more troublesome behavior for parents and teachers to cope with, the latter is by far the most damaging to the child involved.

Statistics help to highlight the unhappy reality. Suicide ranks as the third greatest cause of death among American teenagers. Although the suicide rate for the United States as a whole has jumped dramatically, officially accounting for 26,430 deaths in 1975, it has shown its greatest increase in the fifteen-through-college age group. That these youngsters don't really want to die is proven by their methods and the too-often ignored warning signals they try to send out beforehand. Because it seems inconceivable to envious age that one so young and full of promise could possibly be lonely enough to feel this is the only way out, the warning signals are often ignored. There is as well a certain element of disgrace which attaches itself upon the family of a would-be suicide. The reflection upon father or mother is too painful to enable one to take such threats or suggestions seriously and thus to pursue the proper course of help. Death by suicide becomes the ultimate exposure of failure within the family. So, with ambivalant feelings on the part of both child and whoever passes as caretaker, the real causes of alienation often remain muted and uncertain.

What all statistics do point to, however, is the factor of parent loss in the incidence of child suicide. Joseph D. Teicher, director of Child-Adolescent Psychiatric Services of the Southern California Medical Center, declared in *Science News* (De-

cember 30, 1972) that the loss of one or both parents in early
life is the most prevalent cause leading to suicide. There is a
feeling of aloneness in coping with problems of growing up.
Whether the separation be by death or voluntarily by divorce,
the trauma is evident. Either circumstance was present in 72
percent of those attempts studied. Where there was subsequent
replacement of a parent, 84 percent felt that they were unwanted by the new mother or father.

Or the child may have a parent—perhaps even both. As with
inner-city loneliness, the physical presence of someone who
should care—but doesn't—merely accentuates the feeling of
unrelatedness. If there is no communication, or if there is ex-
treme permissiveness, the feeling of personal worthlessness is
strengthened. The cry for help is often not so clearly stated as
in the suicide note of a fourteen-year-old: "Dear mom and dad,
I hate you. Love, Billy." They rarely want to *die,* these lonely
children, but they do want to *live*—differently.

The quest for a better quality of life is basically the prime aim
and objective of every tenant of this restless planet. As Thomas
Wolfe said, in *The Hills Beyond* ". . . loneliness, far from being
a rare and curious phenomenon . . . is the central and inevitable
fact of human existence. . . . The final cause of (man's) complaint is loneliness." That so many human beings pursue unworthy goals or ways of achieving the goals meant to satisfy the
inner longing for identity does not alter the fact of its elusive-
ness. The Creator recognized that the material beauties and
benefits of the Garden were not enough. Even God Himself was
not enough. Someone uniquely *of* Adam was needed to give life
a sense of wholeness. Amidst a scene of fragmenting interpersonal relationships, that vast and pitiful edifice, the Tower of
Babel, was undertaken as an insurance against anonymity. Unrelated to their Creator and God, at enmity between themselves, they nevertheless toiled together to make themselves a
name ". . . lest we be scattered" (Genesis 11:4)—alone, without
identity.

But as it was then, so it is today: Man looks to any and every

solution—save those found in Him—to solve his deepest problems. It is, after all, not such a far leap from a twentieth-century
teenager's need for a friend (*any* friend) to the antics of a
Samson trying to impress his contemporaries. Nor is it unbelievable to transpose David, pleasing as he was to God, into a
modern setting, watering his bed with his tears and crying out
in an excess of loneliness, "My God, my God, why hast Thou
forsaken me?"

The cry is universal, the solution very specific and very personal. It is *in Him* that we live and move and have our being.
There begins life and there too lies our sense of direction and
satisfaction—in fact the whole scope of life. If it is true, as
Catherine Marshall said in *To Live Again*, that the Kingdom
of God is a kingdom of right relationships, then the whole
process must surely begin with that relatedness to the Son
which ignites the new life. Only when that relationship is right,
can we truly relate to ourselves and to others. To stand in
Christ's stead and cry a message of reconciliation to a dying
world is not only to minister life but relationship. We bring
"sons" to glory. Too often that message is impersonally given.
Forgotten is the fact that by bringing *sons* we are also creating
brothers. To these newly related brethren in Christ we are to
minister in the bonds of love.

But not only to our spiritual brethren are we to minister life.
There is a link which binds us forever to the totality of Thomas
Wolfe's "manswarm" passing us in the streets. The inescapable
fact for the Christian is that loneliness is one of the great human
needs for which the burden of guilt falls not on the victim but
on his so-called brother. Loneliness is by its very nature an
engine of self-destruction, a paralyzing force, locking its victim
into the ever-more constrictive confines of his own emotional
trauma. Self-pity and a zero-level sense of self-worth finally
mold a personality which is unacceptable to all but the most
charitable. But since charity is the identifying mark of men and
women recreated by the new birth in God's image and charac-

ter, the challenge is clear. Jesus, the Friend of publicans and sinners, of the widow and orphan, of the outcast and rejected, has left His representatives here in His stead. Indwelt and empowered by the Holy Spirit, we are commanded to do His works in His name. That Christians—by a false sense of "separation"—too often withdraw from the uglier aspects of involvement in this world's ills is surely a sad commentary on their own appreciation of Christ's redeeming work in *them*.

As is to be expected, the Bible is full of insights into this gravest of man's ills. The very human characters which parade upon its pages encounter losses and bereavements, victories and defeats, even as we. Only the setting is different. Just as surely as Adam was created in the image of God, so he still lives in the descendents of his race pressing around us in the twentieth century. The image is marred—sometimes scarcely recognizable—and so is the cry. Who will answer? Perhaps a closer look at some of the divinely inspired details of God's lonely people of the Bible will help those who would be responsive to the need as well as those who seek a way out.

2

Someone to Call Your Own

It was pure chaos—an earth formless and void and of an impenetrable darkness. And yet, in all that limitless expanse of watery wilderness and in all that sunless and measureless passage of time from eternity past to eternity future, there was a sense of expectancy—of something meaningful about to arise from utter meaninglessness. Then it came, that moment for which the universe had been waiting. The Spirit of God moved upon the waters, a Voice spoke, and behold there was light.

That primeval illumination rested upon a world still formless and still void, but touched for the first time with the stamp of divine order. What had been until then a shapeless mass of maverick matter, adrift, meaningless, awash in a dead and stifling sea, was now fully exposed in all its terrible desolation. It had to be the first stage—this ruthless exposure that set the scene for the step-by-step imposition of order which would eventually change chaos into a world pleasing to its Maker.

In perfect obedience the new Creation responded to the commands which now issued daily from the heavens. Whether it was the convulsions that divided the waters above and below the firmament, the quickening which carpeted the earth with herbs and grasses, or the ornamenting of the heavens with sun, moon, and stars—the plan progressed in measured stages, each day marking that creative act which culminated in the triumphant benediction: "And God saw that it was good."

At last, no longer formless or void, bathed with the nourishing rays of the sun by day and the gentleness of the moon by night, and lush with an enclosing mantle of green, the earth stands at the dawning of the sixth day. Four times a supremely satisfied Creator has announced His approval. A world of order and harmony is arising from the fingers of God. Why? What does He have in mind? Surely something more than the stark and soulless beauty which had replaced undisciplined chaos. A contemporary poem suggests, "And God stepped out on space, and looked around and said, *'I'm lonely—I'll make me a world . . .'* " (from "The Creation" by James Weldon Johnson).

Certainly God, being perfect and complete in Himself, couldn't experience the loneliness we know. But He did long to bestow His love upon others, and to do so He first had to create a being capable of loving and of being loved. Someone made in His own image. God was fashioning for Himself a very special realm in which to exercise a unique relationship. The Creation of far-flung galaxies with their countless billions of stars, and the unique formation of this tiny water-blessed planet were only in preparation for the greatest creative act of all. Earth would be peopled with creatures fashioned in God's image . . . and angels must have hovered in expectant wonder waiting to see . . . they knew not what.

Without this final purpose fulfilled, a haunting loneliness pervaded the forming universe in spite of God's touch at every step. Nor was it dispelled when the waters "brought forth abundantly" and every winged fowl took to the hitherto empty skies. Nor when the earth became alive with "everything that creepeth." Earth's emptiness had been filled with a great and varied multitude of living things, but still God's heart was not satisfied. What He saw was *good,* but it was incomplete. Still missing was a relationship with a kindred spirit. Beauty and order were not enough, though it was in God's nature that these should grace everything He made. Even the authority which God exercised over His Creation was to be relegated elsewhere when the final act had been completed. And so still the earth waited.

"Let us make man in our image, after our likeness: and let them have dominion. . . ." With those words there is a sense of quickening, of meaning and reason falling into place. There is a sense, too, of the harmony of God's perfect scheme for fellowship with man. Formed of the dust of the earth and infused with the breath of life, man was to be the visible expression of God's own life and character and the one through whom the Creator would exercise dominion on the earth.

God had made man an extension of Himself—in His own "image." Man *belonged* to God in a very unique way. That same sense of belonging exists today thousands of years after the Fall. Augustine's declaration "Thou hast made us for Thyself, O God, and we are restless until we find our rest in Thee" is as true today as it was on the sixth day of Creation. That men still find a life of separation from God as disorienting and emotionally devastating today as at that initial wrench which thrust Adam and Eve from the Garden should hardly be surprising. And that God *desired* the companionship of His creature—and still desires it—should weigh as a wholesome balance against the sense of sin and imperfection which we are bound to feel as fallen beings.

Satisfied at last, God looked on what He had wrought and ". . . behold, it was *very* good." After a day of work Adam expected to be sought among the trees and we can assume he was always available. From later verses we know that there was communion between these two. God's Spirit plumbed the depths of His own image in man's God-breathed spirit, igniting a flaming love that burned from Adam's heart all thought of himself; and from the soul's hearth a warmth and light shone out through Adam's eyes and energized his deeds so that the closely watching angels recognized in this first man the reflection of God's own character.

Yes, God was satisfied. But Adam was not. His environment was beautiful. All its abundance was his to enjoy. He was busy, useful, and "important." All the ingredients were there for the ideal fulfilled life—all but one. He was *alone.* But he had God. They lived in intimate and loving fellowship. You don't hear Adam complaining. But then, how could he? He didn't know what he was missing. The longing that a loving God recognized in Adam was nameless (and faceless) yet. Adam wanted something—something that was definitely missing from the Garden scene, and God knew exactly what it was.

"It is not good that man should be alone."

That declaration of incompleteness is the first negative judgment introduced in the newly created earth. Until now each stage in the ordering of this man-oriented planet had been pronounced *good.* We could hardly say that the infinitely wise God *searched* for a solution to the dilemma of man's loneliness. But certain it is from the biblical account that God's first concern after man's Creation was to find a companion for him. All the species of exotic animals had been paraded before Adam. He had become intimately enough acquainted with them to give each the name that just suited it. Adam in his innocence must have given some tentative substance to his vague longings as he scrutinized each one in turn. Could *this* one be something special in his life? Was that one sufficiently like him to share a bit in life's deeper meanings?

There must have been affection and loyalty. Everyone knows the unconditional love that a dog will give its master, no matter how badly treated or ignored. But it was even more than an apparent love or just being by one's side that was lacking. With nothing to relate that longing to, it must have been with real hope that Adam held court over the animal kingdom and saw them pass in review one by one—but none of them was suited to the need his Creator had built into him. Into the dust of earth God had breathed an energizing spirit that found no response in the animals of the Garden, intelligent and docile and affectionate though they were.

One of the strangest and least understood phenomena is the fact that this same loneliness that Adam felt in the solitude of that new earth still haunts his descendants—all 4 billion of them crowding today's shrunken world. It's a loneliness that neither patient nor psychiatrist can really come to grips with no matter how they try. One has to go back farther than one's own childhood to understand—back to the very beginning.

It was a problem that God understood. He Himself pronounced the verdict: "It is not good. . . ." Adam, on the other hand, like his modern descendants, had no way of understanding it though he felt it. And so it is today. We scarcely know *what* to pray for, or *how* to pray as we ought, so nebulous do some of our deepest longings seem. Into that vacuum steps the Holy Spirit to intercede before the Father with groanings which can't find expression in words.

Adam waits. Other needs had been supplied (which at that stage he didn't have the capacity to appreciate). He had a relationship with God. It was first in importance. There was a reassuring sense of control and direction. There was security. There was love, companionship. Then, too, all the necessities of life were supplied. Every tree that was good for food—a veritable gastronome of good eating—was at his disposal. In fact, the whole Garden had been planned with Adam in mind. The esthetic pleasures hadn't been overlooked. He was surrounded by a beauty totally untouched by the mark of death or decay. Every tree that was pleasant to the sight had taken root here at the express command of God for Adam's enjoyment. Last of all Adam had a job. It was one of tremendous responsibility but with commensurate rewards. Placed in the Garden to dress it and to keep it, he was earth's first ecologist. If ever there was a perfect setup, this should have been it. But there was still that indefinable something. . . .

Having experienced God's loving provision in so many ways, Adam waits. It's at this point that Adam could have done what we so often do. Agreeing with God's verdict, he could have gone ahead to try to solve his own problem. Perhaps there was some creature God had overlooked—something as yet unexplored beyond the Garden that would satisfy the empti ness. . . . But, no, he waits and by so doing sets the stage for the last act to be played out in the drama of God's perfect Creation.

The Fall could have taken place right here, as it so often does in our own lives. We're lonely. It's not good to be alone. Human nature rebels against it and God Himself has declared it "not good." An anguished cry gives vent to our pent-up feelings.

"I *must* have a friend . . . a wife . . . a husband . . . *now*. It's the only way I can be happy!"

"Yes," replies the Father, who knows it even better than we. "I'll give you one. Wait."

But so often we find it hard to wait because we lack that confidence in God's love that assures us He knows best. So we proceed to "help" God find the solution instead of waiting for His perfect filling of that void. Disastrous marriages and spiritually debilitating friendships without number have been the result. Too late we learn that the difference between God's choice to fill the empty heart and our own is big enough to make the waiting worthwhile.

Mercifully for Adam, the trust that had until now responded in harmony to God's wise direction caused him to fall into a "deep sleep." What a contrast between that trusting sleep and the tranquilizer-suppressed inner tensions and strident demands for "fulfillment" we hear today, whether personal or on a national scale. There was an aching loneliness to be cured— a void to be filled. God knew it and promised relief. Though Adam didn't understand, he gave himself up in total confidence to the One who knew and sympathized with his need infinitely better than he could himself.

What God fashioned during that deep sleep was something totally new in the art of Creation. The beasts and birds and everything else had been formed from the dust of the earth. But although Adam, too, had come from the dust, he felt no relationship to any of these. The spark of recognition just wasn't there. But now God takes—not more dust—but part of Adam —a rib—and from that. . . .

When Adam awoke, there in new-born beauty stood a girl whom he instantly recognized. She was part of himself. Those eyes mirrored his own soul. The spirit which emanated from that warm flesh was God-breathed like his own. The body itself aroused a response within him that was like nothing he had ever experienced. Adam's heart leaped, and he cried, "This is now bone of my bones, and flesh of my flesh: she shall be called Woman, because she was taken out of Man."

Science has no better explanation. The mathematical odds worked out on computers are so overwhelming that only the most stubbornly prejudiced still cling to the fantasy that man and woman each evolved into the perfect complement of the other. In *The Difference of Man and the Difference It Makes,* Mortimer J. Adler shows that man differs in *kind,* not just in degree, from all animals—with a chasm between that no evolutionary process could possibly bridge. Far from the male chauvinism that advocates of Women's Lib claim to detect in the biblical account, Eve's Creation was not an afterthought, but the climax planned by God. Adam was incomplete without her, and she without him; and both were incomplete without God. As their relationship with the Giver and Sustainer of all life was to be one of love and trust, so it was to be with each other. The love that suddenly made Adam's pulse pound was not to be a possessive one ("She is *mine!*")—but much deeper and infinitely more satisfying than mere possession. "She is *me!*" Adam must have exulted. Christ's command is for the man to love his wife as his own flesh. It makes sense. Their flesh *is one.*

A whole new world had opened up to Adam. That certain feeling he'd had could be named now. It was called *loneliness*. At last the ideal environment, the good living, the executive job, status as God's friend—it could all be savored to the fullest because he had someone to share it with him. For a time, at least, the Garden was a Paradise not only of beauty and plenty, but also of love. Unfortunately for the honeymooning couple the perfection they enjoyed was soon to be lost, and once again that sense of aloneness would stalk its victims among the trees. Paradise would be shattered. All man's attempts since then to glue the broken pieces back together—or to build a bigger and better Paradise with technology—have proven futile. Now surrounded by the shining steel, plastic, and miracle fabrics of his brave new world, modern man is still alone and afraid.

We are reviewing what happened to Adam and Eve not just to entertain ourselves with a fascinating old story, but to pursue a cure for loneliness today. Adam had lost a rib—but by that loss he'd gained something of infinitely greater value. When he first felt the empty place in his left side and then looked into Eve's lovely eyes he must have smiled with satisfaction. That diminishing of his own body had enhanced his life. He had really gained his own self back again, but in a more complete and a more beautiful form. Little wonder that our fathers, in a more gallant age, spoke of their wives as "the better half." Perhaps the words were a bit patronizing—something to call the wife besides "the little woman"—but God intended the exchange to be a generous one. In wide-eyed wonder Adam beheld what God had wrought from his useless rib.

And so it is when we give ourselves in love to others. Whatever the sacrifice is, the gain is so much greater. "It is better to give than to receive." We all know the principle, but those who practice it know also that they receive far more than they give. And here we hit upon something of paramount importance: giving of ourselves to others is really one of the best cures for

loneliness. It worked for Adam, and it will work for his children
—if God is in control.

"I'm so lonely . . . why don't people remember *me,* befriend
me, care about *me?"* Most of us are too sophisticated to express
our loneliness in such candidly selfish terms—but who can
honestly deny ever having used these very words in the secret
of his own heart? Loneliness always turns one inward. To be
free, one must turn outward away from self to others. But
there's a secret. Kind words, material gifts, money, even precious time given to others will not bring the longed-for deliverance. One can be ever so active, and seldom alone, yet still be
frighteningly lonely. Let go of that rib. Give of yourself to
others—you're not the only lonely one—and see if you don't
find yourself falling blissfully asleep in God's arms, and when
you have awakened, you—like Adam—will be joyfully surprised to see what He has made out of that little bit of yourself
you've given away.

Do they sound lonely, those two in the Garden? It's not so
much the number of friends but rather the quality that makes
for fulfillment. When two are compatible, they're sufficient to
each other's needs. We can assume there wasn't a difficult
period of adjustment. No carbon copies of each other, these two
had complementary natures that fused into one harmonizing
whole.

But already Adam must have known that it wouldn't always
be just the two of them, so he lays that very sound principle
squarely on the line: "Therefore shall a man leave his father and
his mother, and shall cleave unto his wife. . . ." These were the
words of a man supremely satisfied and one who expected to
stay that way.

Did you ever wonder what kind of a home Adam and Eve
had? It couldn't have been much, that home in a garden. Food
for the plucking and a fragrant bed of grass. That was all.

"The faucet's leaking again, Adam! When will you get
around to it?" Such words were never heard.

"Another button off my shirt! What do you *do* to them, Eve?"

Never.

So just what did they do? We're not told. Only that Adam had a helper adequate for his needs and Eve had someone whose instant adoration she'd inspired. Without socks to darn or clothes to iron—nothing, in short, to *make*—Eve was a homemaker nevertheless.

And Adam? The zoo keeper extraordinary who commanded the animals and subdued the earth comes home, not to dominate but to communicate with his wife. Dominion he had known before and knew it still, but it had never dispelled the loneliness for him. Only communion with someone uniquely a part of himself could do that. Now he had someone to talk with. What he felt within could be shared with someone else who would feel it too. He had someone who cared for him as he cared for her. God's presence was as intimate as ever. The animals followed him about and nuzzled his hand as always. But these two—the miracle handiwork of God—*belonged.* They belonged first of all to God by right of Creation. They belonged also to one another by virtue of that presentation which had made of each a gift to the other.

Today's new concept of freedom misses it so completely here. The need is not to belong to oneself, but to someone other than oneself. Not to be loved but to love. Before Eve's Creation Adam had had plenty of the independent life. Other than the day's work and the evening report to the Head Gardener, his time was his own. He could feast—*alone.* There was swimming —*alone*—in any of the four magnificent rivers which flowed through Eden. There was the sheer beauty of the Garden or a flaming sunset to enjoy—*alone.* There was no one to interfere with Adam's whims or wants, and God dismisses it all with one word—*alone.*

We don't know how long the happiness lasted. Adam was the world leader (under God) who feared neither wars, famine, nor

the electorate. It was his world—and Eve's. She was the First
Lady in more ways than one. Everything was perfect! Words
cannot describe the exquisite joy of companionship these two
shared day after glorious day. There was no selfishness, no
jealousy, no touchiness nor fear that the other might take advantage—but a perfect trust and a love that gave and gave and
gave without demanding anything in return. Little did either of
them suspect that this satisfying sense of belonging to each
other was the overflowing of God's love through His Spirit's
dwelling within them. They thought this love was their own and
would never end.

But one day the loneliness descended again, this time on both
of them. In one instant of disobedience, what intimate fellowship they had enjoyed with God was shattered. Vaguely they
had expected something of the kind as the price they would
have to pay for their new so-called freedom. But they were
startled to sense an alienation from each other and even from
themselves. Feeling fractured inside, and afraid of they knew
not what, Adam and Eve tried to hide among the trees, not only
embarrassed at the thought of facing God, but ashamed to look
at one another.

"Where are you?"

All nature must have stopped at the words. Isaiah speaks of
the mountains singing and the trees clapping their hands in a
future day. Perhaps such a celestial concert had been part of the
joys of that Garden paradise. If that's the case, Lohengrin could
never compete with the wedding processional that must have
accompanied God's presentation of the newly formed Eve to
Adam. But now that music had been stilled; and in that deathly
silence a voice calls out again.

"Where are you, Adam?"

Didn't God know? Of course He did. And Adam knew that
He knew. His impulse—the impulse of guilt—was to hide.
God's purpose was to find him and to bring him back.

The question was really, "Where are you, Adam, in relation

to Me?" And Adam, totally and instantly cut loose from a relationship that had given meaning to every element of life, can't bear to answer the question.

"I heard Your voice. . . ."

"That's great—the way it should be, Adam."

". . . and I was afraid. . . ."

"Of your *friend,* Adam?"

". . . because I was naked. . . ."

"So . . . haven't you always been?"

". . . and I hid myself."

"From *Me,* Adam? You know that's impossible!"

Now, for the first time, Adam knew real loneliness—the loneliness of separation from God—and his very soul throbbed with an ache far worse than that emptiness he'd felt before the creation of Eve. A thousand Eves could never satisfy him now, as King Solomon would one day discover in his pursuit of vanity. Until that relationship with God was restored, the whole Creation would groan in pain because dominion had now passed from Adam (and his descendants) to Satan; and man would struggle through a hard existence alienated not just from his environment and his fellows but also from his real self, which he had lost when God's Spirit had withdrawn from his spirit and taken away the image in which man had been created.

Every element of the ultimate loneliness that plagues modern man is here. We still hear God's call, "Where are you in relation to Me?" and we're bothered—terribly. We search everywhere to find an answer that isn't really an answer to the painful question. There's that God-given impulse to recognize God's claim on our lives, but in guilty fear we run for cover, knowing full well there is no hiding place from the loving search.

Poor Adam was really rather transparent—not yet a very accomplished sinner. He couldn't have imagined for a moment that the One who had by a word of command planted each tree Himself didn't know exactly where he and Eve were cowering. His instant nonanswer gave away his eagerness to be found. If he'd really thought he was making a successful getaway he'd have remained quiet.

And when the excuses for the pitiful escape started tumbling out, Adam exposed himself as surely as if his hastily fashioned apron were disintegrating leaf by leaf. "I was naked" was just another way of saying, "I see myself as I am—sinful—and I don't want anyone else to see me like this." The unnecessary announcement, "I hid myself," could as well have come out as, "Thou O God seest me, and I'm really relieved that You do."

Indeed, in spite of the covering they'd made for themselves, Adam and Eve are left feeling more naked by the minute. Cut off from God, they have become totally disoriented in their relationship with each other as well. One member of that animal kingdom, which was to be part of man's dominion, has managed to beguile Eve, who in turn has used her femininity to seduce Adam into sinning against God's one edict.

From the loneliness of guilt the drama moves to the loneliness of expulsion. It was "not good to be alone" in failure any more than in success. Their mouths had been stopped and they took their places as guilty before God, but it would be too much to expect that our first parents didn't indulge in a little recrimination once they'd been driven out of the Garden.

"Now look what you've done, Adam!"

"*Me! You* started it, Eve!"

"Well, you didn't have to just go along with everything. If you hadn't encouraged me. . . ."

"Well, that line you fed me: 'good, pleasant, make me wise. . . .' See if I *ever* listen to you again!"

"Watch it, Adam. Your apron's slipping. . . ."

Everything was different now. That sheltering earth-womb from which Adam had been formed was now hostile and threatening, hiding a thousand dangers and potential disasters. What had once been its ready bounty had to be taken by much labor and force. Man was meant to live intimately with nature. He was *of* the earth. The wages of sin would one day send him back to the earth. But in the unhappy and uncertain interval he must learn to conquer and make fruitful a world upon which the sentence of death had as obviously fallen as upon himself. Of course a loving God did find a way to reestablish contact with Adam. Beneath the shelter of the blood sacrifice they could again communicate. But his environment was never the same again for Adam, nor was his fellowship with Eve; and the consequences linger to this day.

In the Garden nature hadn't been an alien and a fearful thing. There'd been no conflict there. But modern man stands in awe before Mount Everest, Victoria Falls, the Grand Canyon. There is a mystique, a power, a fearsome and indefinable something that draws and yet repels. Man isn't quite comfortable pitting his small self against such awesome grandeur. That strange relationship of mutual enmity between himself and his environment that Adam first experienced is clearly reflected in Admiral Byrd's description of an Antarctic blizzard he endured during those incredible six months spent alone on the polar ice. "... *extravagantly insensate* ... in its *vindictiveness*. ... The whole *malevolent rush* is concentrated upon you as a *personal enemy*. In the *senseless explosion* of sound, you are *reduced to a crawling thing* on the margin of a *disintegrating world* ..." (from *Alone* by Richard E. Byrd).

With man's expulsion from the Garden's comfortable familiarity came the impulse to band together in cities to show a united front against what had now become the lonely "out there." Again and again man is drawn, however, to his primitive origins—never quite at home there—never quite at home away from it.

In our day we're seeing a revival of the nature cult. The fact that it has all the elements of a cult would indicate how alien man still feels in his own environment. Even as man changes the face of the earth with his cities and freeways and industrial complexes, he tries to stem the dehumanizing tide with his organically grown potatoes and his Earth Borne shampooed hair. But he can *never* recapture the easy familiarity he once had with his environment. Ecology has become a top priority —but many experts feel we have awakened too late. Too late, indeed, for the point of no return was passed in that Garden at the dawn of history. The only hope now is a new universe made by God; and this is exactly what He has promised to those who will surrender themselves into His hands to let Him make them over again too.

Poor Adam. He lost so much. Today's Adam and his Eve are slipping ever further behind in the search for the lost Eden. Cut off from life itself by his own unwillingness to come to terms with his Creator—estranged from his lovely Eve—alienated from the earth and its intended abundance—man wanders, adrift on a speck of dust he calls earth, lost somewhere in the vast cosmos of space. Alone.

"Where are you?" rings the cry of the Seeker.

Afraid, vulnerable, guilty, alone—today's Adam and his Eve can scarcely conceal their eagerness to be found.

3

"Why This, Lord?"

Across the desert the three camels plodded, each with its solemn-visaged passenger swaying in time with the rhythmical gait of his mount. Conversation was sporadic, and when these three did speak it was to return again and again in tones of disbelief to what was obviously a well-worn topic.

"Incredible . . . richest man in Uz . . . wiped out! Who would have believed it?"

"But why? That's the question. He always seemed so upright. Never a breath of scandal. Well, there's surely more to this than meets the eye! What do you say, Eliphaz?"

A bony hand reached out to draw the protective *kafiyeh* closer against the glitter of deep-set eyes. "I tremble when I remember how God once came to me in a vision. In this, too, God has given me to understand mysteries. Woe is Job . . . woe . . . woe. Evil will be found out . . . dark evil. Never yet did such calamities befall an innocent man!"

"Yes, yes. You're quite right—as usual. But what a blessed privilege will be ours to comfort our friend. . . ."

"And to be used of God to chasten him. Don't forget that, Zophar!"

Virtue enveloped the three desert princes like a cloak as again they lapsed into contemplative silence. Soon they'd have the details. And from the very lips of Job himself.

Still a day's journey away sat the object of their concern, in a heap of ashes, scraping the running sores of his prurient flesh with a potsherd. He sat alone. The few who passed by stared in disbelief. Could this be Job? He of the seven thousand sheep, the three thousand camels, the five hundred yoke of oxen and the five hundred she-asses? Who hadn't at least *heard* of the bounty of his table, the magnificence of his chariot, the refinements of his life-style? Granted, his sons and daughters might have been insufferable snobs—the children of the privileged often were—but against Job no breath of scandal had ever stirred. Wealth and influence rested so gracefully on his shoulders. Nothing overbearing or proud or the least bit condescending about Job. Success seemed to suit him so well—the bountiful hand, the gracious manner, the easy self-assurance. But that was just it. Maybe he'd been just a little *too* good to be true. It had been suggested here and there. Could you really trust a man who never slipped up on *anything?*

"I'm going to absolutely *die* of humiliation!" The words wobbled out of control in a rising crescendo. "A spectacle! That's what you are—a spectacle! Don't you have any pride? Think of me . . . your wife . . . at least!"

"Peace, woman . . . peace."

". . . old fool! Sitting there with that sanctimonious look on your face. Curse God! Curse God and die!" With a swish of her robe Job's wife turned on her heel.

Hauran's former supersuccess, moneybags, social lion, honored family man, sat in a pile of ashes—utterly alone. He was a complete washout. How could he begin to assess what he'd lost? That's what bothered him. There was plenty of time to think now. No servants to command. They'd been slaughtered by the Sabeans. No camel caravans to expedite. The Chaldeans had run off with both camels and goods. No children to find comfort in or even to pray for. The roof had caved in and wiped out the hope of his old age. And if that wasn't enough, he had these loathsome boils—these stinking, running, leprous sores. His own wife couldn't stand the sight of him—or the smell. But had she ever—really? And his friends. Where were they? No one came near him. Well, that wasn't entirely the case. He'd seen the thinly veiled curiosity, the stolen glances as they passed by—had seen the quickly averted eye, heard the whispers, the conjectures.

"Do you suppose . . . hmm . . . maybe not everything he *seemed* to be?"

"Job . . . of all people . . . I wonder . . . there has to be something behind it!"

Job felt like a clinical case. "How will this man react?" That was the question on every lip. What was his tolerance level? Did they come to stare and shake their heads because they *cared?* It bothered him. Everybody loves a winner. What did he have to offer now except his integrity? Was it worth something in the eyes of his friends? Was it worth enough? Who were his friends?

From the anguish of his position as the first gentleman of Hauran, Job cries out, "The Lord gave, and the Lord hath taken away. Blessed be the name of the Lord."

My, how good it felt to have said that. It was impressive. He'd seen the unmistakable surprise in the faces of the passersby—and admiration. But he'd meant it, too. He really had. That was a comfort.

What did he have left? Still the careful husbandman of his assets, Job could number them on one finger—his integrity. Oh, yes, there was his wife, forever yakking in the background. *She* was as healthy as ever she'd been before all these calamities had befallen him. From all the raiding forays and collapsing rooftops she'd emerged unscathed—and much, much more vocal. Once there'd been a proper respect, a certain distance that kept the intimacies of marriage from becoming too oppressive. But now, ostracized from his house, it was desperately embarrassing to be so raucously addressed in the very streets of his own city. If only Bildad were here. Or Eliphaz. Zophar. Someone on his own level to commiserate with him. . . .

We're told that Job is the oldest book of the Bible, but it wouldn't be hard to imagine the whole pitiful story taking place in the twentieth century. Bill, such a great fellow—Chamber of Commerce, Lions, Rotary, church and scout leader, photogenic kids, charming wife—wakes up to find that the aerospace industry no longer considers him indispensable. And with the job goes the mortgaged-to-the-hilt, straight-out-of *Better Homes and Gardens* house. And the kids he'd taken such pride in, they've taken off to do their own thing. No sympathy. No understanding. No gratitude for all the sacrifices. The wife? She's something else. "How could you have let this happen? You should have asserted yourself! Don't you have any consideration for *me?* No guts? You could at least have put up a fight!" The final words are flung through the closing door.

For the first time in their lives, Job and Bill are both confronted with a unique loneliness. They're used to success. Friendship (or what had passed for friendship) had come so easily. How superficial these relationships had been was only discovered too late, when they were really needed. Having lost everything else, Job and Bill reach out to lean on friends who seem more inclined to blame than to help. The whole world has turned against them, or so it seems; and if Bill is a Christian, then, like Job, he feels abandoned also by God—and that sense of aloneness is the most devastating of all.

Job didn't realize it, but his case had been determined by a heavenly drama long before the first Sabeans laid a hand upon his oxen. Those two arch antagonists, Satan and God, both had designs upon Job. "A perfect and an upright man" was certainly a worthy addition to the ranks of the righteous. The capture of such a trophy would be a major victory for Satan. And so they bargained for Job—but his reaction would be the deciding factor in this deadly contest.

"Ever notice Job? He's one in a million. Nobody like him."

"Job is good because he's got no reason to be bad."

"We'll see about that. Go to work on him. Anything short of laying a hand on his person."

Round One went to God. With rent mantle and shaven head Job worshiped and blessed his Maker.

"Have you noticed, Satan? Job's still hanging in there."

"So? Try him where it really hurts. Let me give him a whopping case of boils. He'll yell *uncle.*"

"He's yours. Just spare his life."

Round Two wasn't quite such a clear-cut victory. "Shall we accept good from God but not be willing to accept evil?" It had taken quite an effort to get that one out. This time all poor Job could manage was not to "sin with his lips." Before the little knot of observers who lingered by the roadway, Job's integrity had remained intact. He could comfort himself with that anyway.

This terrible feeling of isolation aggravated the problem beyond all endurance. There was no one to consult. In just this way Hamlet would one day sit on a dizzy parapet of Helsingor Castle and soliloquize:

> Whether 'tis nobler in the mind to suffer
> The slings and arrows of outrageous fortune,
> Or to take arms against a sea of troubles
> And by opposing end them?

Hamlet's dilemma was whether to oppose or to accept. Job had neither option.

How he longed for someone who would really sympathize. There was no cure for the repulsive form of leprosy which afflicted him. But for his wounded feelings there were definite possibilities. If only Zophar were there, the nimble-witted, incisive philosopher with all the answers on the tip of his tongue. Or perhaps the learned Bildad. *There* was a man who could put his finger on the problem. At least he was on his level. As for Eliphaz—a bit weird, thanks to a certain metaphysical bent—

he was a worthy protagonist nevertheless.

Well, bless them, they *did* come. And had the grace to sit in silence on the ground beside him for the space of seven days. With rent mantles and dust-sprinkled heads they sat and mourned the tragedy of their great and good friend.

Then, as from a floodgate, Job's pent-up feelings gushed out. "O why was I ever born? Never has *anyone* suffered like me. Why doesn't God just finish the job? There's no hope anyway. Can you, my friends, tell me one little thing that I've erred in? No. That's what I thought. So why this? Why? Why? Why?"

Job settled back, gasping for breath. It had been quite a speech and now he awaited the soothing balm that was sure to come from the lips of his three friends.

"Does God make mistakes? Are you not suggesting that? Now Job, if you were pure and upright He'd be going to bat for you. God's on the side of good, not evil. You know that, Job. Better repent, whatever's on your conscience. . . ."

The oily voice droned on. It wasn't easy to take, this first speech from his so-called friends. In fact, it was stunning . . . unbelievable. But there was more to come—*much more.*

"God is probably not being as hard on you as you deserve."

"This is too much! Who has ever accused me of anything?"

"Words, words. Talk doesn't justify. Who ever perished being innocent?"

"Now wait a minute! You think you know everything . . . ? Tell me exactly where I've erred."

"All right. You're a liar."

". . . and wicked."

"Your belly is full of the east wind!"

"You're crafty."

". . . abominable."

". . . filthy!"

Poor Job. By this time he was reeling. Like a punch-drunk boxer dodging blows, he winced, ducked, maneuvered—all to no avail.

"A fine bunch of comforters you are . . . the whole lot of you! I looked for a little pity. It's not just my friends who've turned against me. The hand of *God* is against me. Do you know what that means? Well, let me tell you one thing. He's not going to let me down after all. I'll see Him some day. With my own eyes. Even if I rot. I *know* it."

The debate had hardly begun. Day after day Job got skewered, basted, and roasted. And still he stuck to his guns. It had become a local *cause celebre.* Who couldn't admire the determination of that disease-ridden heap? And who could fail to be impressed by the finely turned phrases of the three desert chieftains who'd come so far to set their friend straight?

Job was a good man. God plainly says so. There was none like him—perfect, upright, God-fearing. Then why all this? Surely his anguished cry was legitimate. Philosophers of our own day voice the same *Why?:* and receiving no answer from the silent heavens, they declare man's existence and death a macabre joke. Man is pictured adrift on a polar sea—isolated, alone. Job's cry is the wail of earth's first existentialist: "I've been stripped, destroyed, estranged from my family, forgotten by friends, alienated from my wife, despised by my children, abhorred by all. Life is definitely a bad joke."

Who could blame Job? Yet, at the very end of the bitter recital, he declares his assurance that one day he'll see God in a restored state. Could we suggest that life hung in the balance on this delicate point? The poor man needed sympathy badly, or at least he was dead sure he did. And what did that sympathy revolve on? An acknowledgment of his integrity. But it wasn't forthcoming, and in an excess of frustrated need, Job lashes out with his grandiose declaration. It was a beautiful statement— granted—but one which Job wasn't ready for quite yet; for how to reconcile the Redeemer he longed for with the integrity he insisted was his? Redemption avails only *for sinners.*

Job, Job. Your fig leaves are slipping. How like your father you are—Adam, that is. But with you it's words instead of

leaves. God calls as he did to Adam. "Where are you, Job—
behind all those words?"

A God of "ways that are past finding out" was dealing with
a man of whom it could be said "there was none like him in all
the earth," in order to establish with him a proper relationship.
God knew His man could take this benevolent ruthlessness. The
woman caught in adultery knew she was a sinner. Because she
was convinced already and wearing no fig leaves, Jesus could
begin the gracious work of covering immediately. For Job, the
medicine had to be stronger.

For all of us one of the most excruciating forms of loneliness
is the exposure that comes when one's sense of personal integrity is shattered. Loss of a job, marital failure, financial disaster,
prolonged illness—whatever the tragedy that overtakes us—
friends we once counted upon raise questions that imply the
whole thing is our fault. We didn't have enough faith, they
suggest, or God is punishing us for something we need to
confess—and we have the feeling of cowering alone, with the
whole world pointing its collective finger accusingly in our face.
Almost the totality of Job's discourse is directed toward gathering up the bits and tatters of shattered reputation. In C. S.
Lewis's masterful allegory on hell *The Great Divorce,* he has his
characters go to ludicrous lengths to give valid excuses for their
being caught in that embarrassing place. Similarly the story is
related of the king who wished to show a special mercy by
offering freedom to the prisoner who would acknowledge the
justice of his sentence. Predictably his offer went begging.

One day every mouth shall be stopped and all the world stand
guilty before God. In the meantime the world is a vast garment
manufacturers' union. With words as fragile as leaves, men try
to cover the loneliness of self-exposure. Even as Job protests his
integrity, he leaves himself a loophole: "All right, if you're
going to be that way, I'll have you know that God will justify
me some day. My Redeemer lives." And with that contradic-
tion he exposes his wretched nakedness even further.

The intolerable burden of acting what one is not robs oneself not only of the companionship of one's real self, but of God's fellowship as well. Painful as it was, Job had to come to a right evaluation of himself. All the self-views that the psychiatrists try to root out as neurotic and introspective and sick are just the first step to deliverance. The anguished cry "I abhor myself, and repent in dust and ashes" was wrung from Job's lips in an instant of wonder at the beauty and righteousness and majesty of God. A proper self-evaluation depends upon an honest admission of one's total dependence upon the Creator for everything. Without that, Job's relationship with God could never be a personal one. Every earthly friend had failed him—but there was one Friend into whose everlasting arms he could fall and find comfort and security—if he was only willing to trust Him in spite of everything that had happened.

The real root of loneliness is the lack of a right relationship with God, although it takes some of us a long time to see this. Before disaster struck, Job's attitude toward God seemed to be that of one successful man toward another. Job knew nothing of grace or forgiveness because he didn't think he needed either. Having been "perfect" and self-sufficient, no one—not even God—could share his sorrow in disaster. The intolerable burden had to be carried alone.

His plastic armor of self-confidence shattered at last, Job discovered in misery what he had been blind to in prosperity —that he was alone, utterly and unbearably alone. And with that realization a mask seemed to fall off, leaving the real Job exposed to himself and to his friends. Like Adam and Eve, Job was shocked by his nakedness and tried desperately to cover himself with protestations of his blameless perfection.

How different was David's experience in the Valley of the Shadow of Death. "Thou art with me!" he cries joyfully. He knew this comforting Presence because he had already confessed, "Thou, O God, seest me," exactly for what I am. Fearful often, admittedly discouraged, forsaken by friends, pursued relentlessly by his enemies, but "Thou art *with* me!" It was the comfortable feeling of living with the real David and the supreme security of knowing the forgiveness of his gracious Friend.

Job's apron slipped badly when he whimpered, "That which I so greatly feared is come upon me." Afraid and insecure while feasting with his companions in his high-ceiled house? Yes, indeed—but no one had ever suspected that his confident smile and gracious manner were so much camouflage hiding the real Job, a man unknown to his closest friends. At last the secret he'd guarded so carefully—the one he'd been afraid to admit even to himself—was out. And his confessed fear of losing wealth and health was an admission that self-righteousness is a burden too great for any man to bear. Not knowing God's grace because he didn't really know God or himself, Job imagined that success and prosperity and a beautiful family were God's reward for his meticulous practice of good instead of evil —and so he was forever apprehensive that if he slipped God would angrily pull the rug out from under him.

But he *hadn't* slipped—at least he couldn't see where. Yet God had taken everything away. Choked with anguish at the thought of such injustice, Job wails in self-righteous indignation, "I put on righteousness and it clothed me." Yes, Job was righteous; there was "none like him in all the earth"—but it was his own righteousness, not God's. And that's why he lived in constant fear, always repairing his apron of good deeds because of a nagging suspicion that it wasn't fully covering him at some vital spot. The corrosive fear of exposure had gripped him long before the first Sabeans began sniping away at his security blanket of wealth and power. Now stripped of that, he feels horribly alone, without comforter or friend—never suspecting that this loneliness he feels is really the first necessary step if he is ever to know God.

"If the One you preach is a God of love, then why . . . ?" How many arguments are begun with just those words! It was basically Job's hang-up. The pain of being forsaken by a God whom he'd scrupulously served was unbearable. Not knowing God well enough to assess His real character and discovering that his fine friends were left totally unconvinced by his so meticulously documented virtue, Job feels a new sense of aloneness—the communication gap has isolated him from a God who won't answer and from supposed friends who don't understand. Offended because no one will play the game by his rules, Job decides to give the whole world the silent treatment, and in the hurt voice of a self-styled martyr he cries, "The words of Job are ended."

Job's God, who has been patiently waiting for his storm of self-justifying words to subside, now speaks out of this silence and at last Job begins to understand the why of this whole painful experience. Far from being the offscouring of a capricious God's disfavor, Job was the central object of a heavenly contest of cosmic proportions. Like all of us, Job's success—and Job's misery—filled the universe for him. "I cry unto thee, and thou dost not hear me . . . thou regardest me not . . . thou art cruel to me!" Little did Job suspect how important he really was—so important that he was the subject of debate between the two greatest superpowers in the universe. Job—good, patient, righteous Job—was to be a demonstration before principalities and powers of God's purposes and might. Job thought he'd been abandoned as beneath God's notice, whereas all the while he was participating in something of far-greater magnitude than he could have imagined.

How about you? Is there pain and loneliness of an overwhelming kind? Are you demanding—like Job—an explanation? Have you considered the possibility that it's not chastening or even purifying that God is primarily concerned with (though both may be involved as they were in Job's case)? Remember that nothing, whether it's angels or principalities or powers or things present or things to come, can separate you from God's love (Romans 8:38). You are still in His hands and *in His care.* Believing that, you can trust Him to use the loneliness of disaster and unfaithful or misunderstanding friends to mold you into a closer likeness to Christ. That faith will bring you out to victory no matter how dark it all looks now.

Satan knows very well the quality of Christ's resistance to temptation. They faced one another often, not only during those forty days in the wilderness. "But Satan," God demands, "have you considered My servant Job (or Sue or Amy or Sam)? The Spirit of Christ indwells them. The cross of Christ isn't worth anything if it doesn't avail for them, too. Try them. See for yourself." It's Paul's message to the Ephesians: "To the intent that now unto the principalities and powers in heavenly places might be known by the church the manifold wisdom of God" (3:10).

In this same way you and I can be groomed to demonstrate in the heavenlies before the devouring Adversary that the things of which we speak are truly realities, that He *is* sufficient, that the Blood *does* avail to cleanse and to keep.

What a victory in heavenly places when Job uttered the words, ". . . mine eye seeth thee . . . I repent." After God's righteousness was vindicated and Job was restored, how few verses it took to double every blessing he had lost. Yet even then he could not have known how important a breakthrough of faith he had demonstrated before the roaring lion and the devourer of souls.

And so it is with us in our lonely trials. Yet we have the promise that one day we will "know as we are known" (1 Corinthians 13:12). Then we will see the glorious purpose fulfilled, and be satisfied. "But the God of all grace," said Peter, "who hath called us unto his eternal glory by Christ Jesus, after that ye have suffered a while, make you perfect, establish, strengthen, settle you" (1 Peter 5:10).

We leave Job a new man, secure in his new relationship with God, clothed with a righteousness not his own, and the center of a whole new realm of honest relationships. Rid at last of the old corrosive self-consciousness, the fear of exposure, the compulsive explanations, Job can get on with the job of getting to know God better. What he "so greatly feared" had come to pass, had become history, and had left him with the assurance that his God would never leave or forsake him, nor indeed ever had.

4

Alone at the Top

The year was 1350 B.C. and in the delta lands of Egypt's Nile River the Hebrews had for long years been toiling in the muddy, black fields. Under the hot sun—scorching even in winter—they stooped in back-breaking labor to imbed the seeds under furrowed soil. Then, while waiting for harvest, it was back to brickmaking again. With rigor and in bitterness they were made to trample the sticky mixture of mud and sand and straw and laboriously drawn Nile water, always under the watchful eye and cruel whip of their Egyptian overseers. Those sun-dried bricks would be raised by other slaves, also Hebrew, into the temples and monuments and palaces that would declare the glory and power of Rameses II, Egypt's greatest Pharaoh.

Life had once been good. To Goshen, gift of a line of grateful Pharaohs long since gone, the famine-ravaged family of Jacob had come to live in peace and plenty. They had prospered under a benevolent protectorship, and God's promise to Abraham that one day his descendants would be as numerous as the sands on the seashore was well on its way to fulfillment.

Always, of course, there had been the intention of returning to the Promised Land, but the resolve had wakened with the passage of time. Here they were aliens, it was true, but among so numerous a Hebrew population (and in so hospitable a land), what real motivation had there been to leave while they prospered under the favor of the ruling dynasty? Years went by, and with each new generation God's promise of a land that would be uniquely theirs dimmed.

Then—a revolution, the overthrow of the Semitic line of Pharaohs and the reuniting of Egypt under native rule. Gone was the privileged status. A purge of foreign elements was begun even as Egypt's mightiest Pharaoh conquered Canaan and subdued the Hittite empire. Secure on his borders and at peace at home, Rameses was now free to launch upon the building program that would endure for centuries as a memorial to the glories of his kingdom.

Reduced to slave status—along with all other foreigners within the kingdom—the prolific Hebrews nicely filled the need for a labor force adequate to the ambitious plans afoot. They were tough, used to the stunning severity of Egypt's sun—and expendable. How they multiplied in spite of all! For each one that died under the whip, there seemed ten more—a hundred —replacements. In awesome splendor Rameses' great city grew along the shores of the Nile.

In time, however, disquieting speculations were raised in the palace. Were the Hebrew slaves perhaps too much of a good thing? Egypt's ancient enemies were thoroughly checked outside her borders, but could this population explosion within develop into a potential fifth column? There'd been rumors of sedition, sabotage—or, worse yet—an alliance with the Canaanites. All that Pharaoh had so painstakingly worked for could be wiped out by this rabble majority in their midst.

A man of action, Pharaoh issued his ingenious proclamation: all Hebrew males were to be killed at birth. But the midwives, at the risk of their own lives, disobeyed the desperate decree. A new order was issued, equally as brutal. Every male child born to the Hebrews was to be thrown into the Nile. Now every Egyptian had a real hand in the success of this operation.

Pharaoh was clever enough to place in the people's hands the responsibility for their own survival. The alternative seemed grim enough.

The newborn son of Amram and Jochebed was a beautiful child and, judging from its lusty cries, a sturdy one as well. There'd been no question of treachery on the part of the Hebrew midwife who'd delivered him. Tenderly he'd been brought into the world. The feeling of triumph was always there. Another child. Another son of Abraham, God's chosen seed. For all their suffering and the hopelessness of their lives, it was Pharaoh who was panicking, not they. "As innumerable as the sands on the seashore . . ." God had said. Now here was another.

Its parents sensed immediately that there was something special about this little one. They could see it from the start. He was so perfectly formed, intelligent—and a joy and sorrow at once. What future could there be for him even without the proclamation that made of every birth a doubly fearful ordeal? That fine intelligence and superb body would at best only waste itself in grueling labor. Now, with this new law, it was only a matter of time until its cries attracted attention and their small hut would be surrounded by the vigilantes.

There was just one faint hope, as fragile as the reeds that grew in the nearby river. A child—a goodly one like theirs—found without any identification in a place which the royal family often frequented might excite pity. A child this attractive just *might* appeal to one of those Egyptian nobles whose own wives were not so fruitful. Torn between hope and maternal agony, Moses' mother wove the basket that was to be her baby's only chance for survival.

It was a huge risk. Against that small infant was arrayed the whole weight of the Egyptian Empire. It was God's promise pitted against a fuming Pharaoh's desperate decree. Even as other babies were being sought and found and flung into the waters of the Nile, one tiny, helpless infant was bobbing in its little reed basket among the rushes and water lilies, inching ever nearer to the secluded spot where the royal princess was just then bathing.

Curiosity led to a command. When the basket was brought to her and opened, the princess's heart was captivated. An abandoned baby was enough to excite any female heart, but this one was so perfect in every way, a fitting ornament for the royal household. She *must* have it and the fewer questions asked the better. "Who knows . . . it could be one of those. . . . But no matter. The Pharaoh, my father, is indulgent, and to please me he'd agree to anything. How amusing, really, that I should adopt a child in such a bizarre way."

Other eyes had observed the drama. Hidden among the rushes was a trembling, anxious child of perhaps twelve years. Ready to weep with relief, she must nonchalantly approach the princess and her ladies and make her helpful offer.

"Excuse me. I know someone who'd nurse the baby for you. That is . . . if you're interested." *(O please, God, make it work!)*

"A nurse? Why, yes. Of course I'll need a nurse. I hadn't thought of that." A laugh tinkled pleasantly in the drowsy air.

The arrangements were agreed upon and with wildly beating heart Miriam raced triumphantly back to the little home she'd left such a short time before. For Jochebed, Moses was a gift twice given.

For three years Moses was loved and cherished and nourished in both body and spirit at home. It was so little time to prepare a child for life, but into that young mind and heart were locked, with God's help, those qualities and those memories which were to set him apart for the most monumental task with which God ever commissioned one of His servants.

Set apart. The phrase describes Moses perfectly. *Nothing* about him from birth to death was what one might call normal. Born of slave parents, condemned to die at birth, he had been plucked from death to live the opulent life of a Pharaoh's son. His home was a magnificent brick palace surrounded by cool gardens made colorful and fragrant with jasmine and oleander. There was a pool in which to splash with the other royal children and later the temple school to attend, where he learned to inscribe hieroglyphics on limestone slabs or scrolls of papyrus.

Moses' own realization of just how different he was came later when life grew less confining. Now an attractive and urbane young man of taste and breeding and intelligence, he could observe in the rising capital all the evidence of Egypt's might and affluence. He saw the trading ships with their cargoes from faraway Asia. He admired the magnificent public buildings which reflected the glory of his adoptive father. He saw it all with a justifiable pride. Only now, when he passed the gangs of slaves toiling with weights and pulleys on the ramp of some new monument, or looked out over the ripening grain where the sweating Hebrews labored under the lash, an uncomfortable feeling had begun to inject itself into his thinking. More and more, he realized, "That's where I belong." Somewhere along the Nile his real parents and his brother and sister still lived out their miserable lives, while he luxuriated in the king's palace. Thousands (some even suggested *millions*) of Hebrews were wearing out their lives in this alien land in just the same way. He couldn't shake the thought. Was it right—this easy life he was living? Shouldn't he be identifying with his own people? The day came when he took an irreversible stand that set him forever at enmity with Egypt and at the same time set him apart in a unique way—even from his own people.

Until now, Moses' future had been determined for him, first by his parents and then by the dictates of court life. He had begun to think for himself these days, however, drawing conclusions, making his own decisions, as every maturing young man does. Leaving the palace courtyard and the splendid metropolis far behind one day, Moses went out among the unfamiliar haunts of the Hebrews with the very special intention of observing their grievances. Of course he didn't realize it at the time, but it was the first step on the road back to the Land of Promise,

for what he saw—and did—that day determined the future
course of his life and of his people.

When night fell and he crept back to the shelter of his palace
room, its luxury had become odious to him, for beneath the
desert sand he'd hidden the slain body of an Egyptian he'd seen
mistreating one of his brethren. The very real fear he felt was
no match for the burning indignation that consumed him.
Something had changed for him that day that could never be
reversed.

If he set out the next morning determined to continue on a
holy vendetta against the rapacious Egyptians, he was brought
to an embarrassing halt. Already convinced that "Egyptian was
bad" and "Hebrew was good," he was in for a rude shock. This
time two Israelites were fighting.

"Hold on there!" Moses shouted authoritatively. "You're in
the wrong. Don't strike your brother."

A pause, a sneer. And more blows.

"Stop, I say! You're acting like *Egyptians.*" Surely that was
a telling argument against such behavior.

"Mind your own business. Who are you, anyway? Think
you're going to kill me the way you killed the Egyptian yesterday?"

The way you killed the Egyptian yesterday! His secret was
out. And worse yet, his idealized version of the Hebrew ethic
was shattered into a thousand pieces. Gone was the beautiful
notion of the unspoiled, "noble savage." These were human
beings, after all, with the same failings and foibles as the Egyptians. The difference for Moses was that they were *his* people
nevertheless. Alienated in spirit from the palace, he found himself misunderstood already in this, his very first attempt to
reach out to his own people. The challenge flung at a chagrined
Moses by the sweaty Hebrew was to become a whining refrain
in years to come. "Who made you a prince and a judge over
us?" There'd been no divine commission yet, only this growing
feeling of compassion. And now, to be so rudely rebuffed by a

boorish and unlettered slave. Well—it hurt.

For Moses, flight was the only hope. Never would Pharaoh forgive him. Perhaps there'd been a time when Moses had thought that someday when he himself succeeded to the throne, he'd right the wrongs of his brethren. He'd have the best of two worlds—a continuing life of affluence and ease plus the gratitude of a liberated people. Any such lingering hope was dispelled when the news of Pharaoh's rage raced through the palace. Just in time Moses fled. From court darling to hunted fugitive—forty-eight hours sufficed to turn Moses' life around. An alien within the royal family, mistrusted by his own people, and now struggling through the parched and hostile wilderness of the Sinai, Moses must have wondered whether he indeed belonged anywhere on God's earth.

Among the inhospitable sandstone rocks and the foreign slaves working the copper mines of the Sinai Peninsula there would at least be the anonymity he needed to stay alive. Beyond that, nothing he'd ever learned in life until now would be of any use to him. His miraculous rescue as an infant, his superb education, the refinements of his life-style—it all rose to mock him as he came at last to a halt beside a desert well. Spared for this? He could have been strolling in his perfume-laden garden at this very minute. . . .

As quick to aid the underdog here as in Egypt, Moses endeared himself on the instant to the Midian priest Jethro and certainly to the seven daughters whose rights he so energetically defended against the churlish shepherds. What a catch! *A man* —any kind—was a find in this God-forsaken wilderness—even a nearly useless one like this who didn't know how to milk a goat or raise a tent. Well, he'd learn. Give him time.

And so Moses, once destined for a ruling position in the mightiest kingdom of his day, gratefully accepted hospitality from this seminomadic tribe of tent-dwellers. Hard as it is to believe, the biblical account tells us that he was "content" in the most incompatible surroundings imaginable for a former prince. He should have married a royal princess. Instead, it was simple, work-roughened, grateful Zipporah, the dark-skinned eldest daughter of his benefactor.

The world would call such a man a failure—a total, crashing zilch. He'd already blown his whole future on a Hebrew boor who couldn't care less. Now he'd thrown in his lot with a bunch of people who could have no appreciation of the high ideals coupled with the sense of total uselessness which possessed him. When his firstborn son was laid in his arms, only one name would do—Gershom—for, as Moses exclaimed, "I have been a stranger in a strange land."

The solitary life that Moses led those forty years offered plenty of time for thought. If ever a man was faced with an identity crisis, it must have been he. Neither fully Israelite, nor Egyptian, and certainly not a Midianite, Moses didn't even have a psychiatrist to help him sort it all out. His work certainly wasn't fulfilling nor his marriage what he'd dreamed of. There was nothing emotionally supportive in his background. Was this then God's man, handpicked for a leadership position of such importance—a man so totally alone?

We've been told how vital to a healthy mental balance good relationships are. We've seen in the tragedy of World War II what an aberration in this area can lead to. Removed from personal contact with the people, a Hitler sought identity for himself and a nation through a quest for power. In our own day the side effects of a dangerous isolation on the part of our own head of state shook our nation to its roots. Can this Moses of the insecure infancy, the strangely privileged teen years, the awakened loyalties, the instant rejection by his own people, the change from favored to fugitive status, and finally the marriage of convenience to a desert sheik's daughter—can any of this possibly have fitted him for the great commission he was about to receive?

Since God knew what He was doing, our answer must be *yes* —precisely. In a solitary place God met this simple shepherd.

It was a different Moses from the one who used to stride so confidently through the royal palace, and who had thought to deliver his people by his own abilities. Now he waited out the monotonous years in desert isolation with no one to share the deep passions that still burned within him beneath the surface of contentment. Versed in mathematics and astronomy, a skilled scribe, a city sophisticate, his companions were ignorant tent-dwellers and goatherds, incapable of understanding this stranger in their midst.

This was the misfit that God called to from the burning bush and commissioned at the age of eighty to lead out his persecuted people. Moses' first words, in response to the call, were, "Here am I." His next words, after the magnitude of the task sank in, were, "Who am I?" With Moses they went hand in hand. Here I am, but You couldn't possibly mean *me*. He'd been a failure until now. There was a world of pathos in the question. Who ever heard of a prince-turned-goatherd qualifying for a job like *this?* They'd say, "The Lord never appeared to you . . . not, of all people, to *you!*"

How many today feel this same sense of worthlessness! Hopes were once so high, ambitions so strong, youth and talents so promising—but somehow the years have passed without fulfillment of the once-cherished dreams, leaving bitterness, disillusionment with life, and the feeling that it's too late. What could *I* ever do—now? Rephrase the question and the whole outlook changes: "What can *God* do through me?" With God there are no limitations except our willingness. It is only when we have come to the end of ourselves that we are ready to let Him be our strength. It took Moses eighty years to reach that point. Most of us don't have that much time—and God doesn't need it. *Today* is the day of salvation. If we're ready and willing, He's able.

When Moses stood at last before Pharaoh, he must have felt akin to a modern-day preacher delivering an old-time message. The language is strong: "All have sinned . . . there is none righteous." Certain claims are made: "Therefore if any man be in Christ, he is a new creature." There are promises: "I will never leave thee nor forsake thee." The message is so certain and uncompromising, but there's the nagging question: Will it work? There's one's whole reputation, a career, laid on the line. A secret doubt at this point has caused many a pastor to water down his message. Better to claim little.

No chance for anything like that at Pharaoh's court. Nor at the Red Sea. Having given up his own conniving crusade when he fled Egypt, and having learned how helpless he really was during forty tedious years of nonaccomplishment in the desert of Midian, Moses had also learned that nothing was impossible with his utterly trustworthy God. Moses feared neither the vengefully determined Egyptian army behind nor the impossible barrier of water before. In faith and obedience, with upraised rod, he commanded the Red Sea to open a dry path. It was surely the ultimate test. Leader on the spot, far out on a limb, he stood apart—alone before his God. Cowering in fear and unbelief, over two million Israelites watched. And it worked!

Moses would have been less than human if he weren't profoundly relieved. He broke into a song, and what a song it was. The man who was "slow of speech" led the people in a song of victory while Miriam led the women in a joyful dance. Moses must have exulted in the sight. With his right arm he'd slain one Egyptian back there in the Egypt of his youth. His brave act had left the ones he was trying to benefit unimpressed and had driven him out from the land as an outcast. This day his raised arm had had power with God. Surely the greatest agent of the supernatural the world had yet seen had established his credentials.

Success, however, is only maintained by fighting more battles. Moses had not yet faced the most difficult test. Standing between God and the people, Moses was yet to taste a loneliness far more excruciating than the solitude of desert vigil without compatible companionship. He was yet to learn that being alone at the top can be far worse than any other form of loneliness. Three days after the Red Sea had parted, the people were crying for water, and six weeks later they were accusing him of deliberately trying to destroy them all. The looks of adulation as they'd joined in his victory chorus had turned to doubt, then disappointment, distrust, and now it was all hanging out: "You've brought us here to die." Their miraculous deliverance from bondage had just been a plot to get them away from the "good life" in Egypt. Forgotten, apparently, was the sting of flesh torn by the lash, their murdered infants, the crippling labor. Viewed from the Sinai, Egypt was a paradise; and Moses, once a hero-deliverer, was now the villain with two million crying for his head.

What the future had in store must really have impressed itself upon Moses in living technicolor. Burned by the relentless sun by day and shivering by night, into the wilderness of Shur he turned to trudge across its parched and barren expanse. Where was the song of victory now?

How often for us too the high-water points of a spiritual warfare and victory are followed by periods of dryness. A pastor leads his flock to new heights of sound, biblical spiritual experience. They stand together on the pinnacle. But the victory sours. It's the experience one is depending upon rather than the carefully nurtured spiritual relationship. One by one they slip behind until the Moses among them is exposed as the villain who brought them, not to God in a new way, but to the bitter wells of Marah. It's the risk that every godly pastor takes —the most heartbreaking occupational hazard he faces. "If only we were back in Egypt," the people wail, as they gaze down at the brackish waters. Today's church member would hardly put it in those words, but the message doesn't escape the pastor. "He's upset us all with this superspiritual separation, absolute surrender, all-for-Jesus kick, and *see, it isn't working.*" One can almost detect a certain triumphant tone: ". . . and I *knew* it wouldn't."

It's a sweet feeling to be the darling of the electorate, whether that body is the people of the United States or a Pulpit Committee or the PTA. But God's idea of leadership is a far cry from the giddy rah-rah of a GOP convention. In fact, God's choice in any realm is very seldom the majority's choice. The Way is narrow and few find it. Neither do many care to be "reproved, rebuked or exhorted" (*see* 2 Timothy 4:2) by those set over them. The judgment of this world upon its rejected King is, "We will not have this man to reign over us." Surely the ambassadors of this King can't expect a different reception. Since the servant is not greater than his Master, a part of leadership's price must be the willingness to stand alone—with Christ.

No man could have been more alone with his God than Moses was on Mount Sinai. At least by now he was comfortable in His presence. It must have seemed a long time since he stood in trembling awe before the burning bush. He "drew near" but the people stood "afar off." They wanted it that way and God knew it. Like the Israelites, today's modern congregations often sit with closed Bibles on their laps and demand, "Speak thou with us and we will hear: but let not God speak with us. . . ."

From God's holy presence Moses returned from the mountain to find the people dancing about the golden calf. In a monumental rage he destroyed it, then returned to the mountain for another forty days. We know what a modern-day endurance test a forty-minute prayer meeting is. Moses returned from his forty days with God energized in body and transfigured in spirit, so intimate had been that encounter. It cemented a friendship which was to take Moses in unbroken fellowship over many years to another mountain on the borders of Canaan. He learned something of the sufficiency of God. There'd been the bitterness of being misunderstood back there in Egypt, the loss of both Hebrew home and court position, the feeling of uselessness in the desert of Midian, and now the logistics of moving a mass of wayward and complaining people across an impossible wasteland to a land they weren't sure they really wanted after all.

Moses had missed out on a lot of things in life. It hadn't been normal in any way. He'd lived the life of a public servant with its scant praise and liberal blame. He'd been willing to be a faithful mouthpiece for God and take the consequences. But there was one thing that had made it all tolerable for him. It had been an exchange back there at Sinai and it went something like this.

"Now, Lord, You've told me to lead these people, but You'll have to show me how."

"My presence will be with you. Count on it."

"Please, if You're not with us, don't let us move an inch from here. It's the only way to go."

"For My good friend, I'll do it. That's a promise."

Here was Moses' secret—*his* antidote to loneliness. "Don't let me go *anywhere* unless You're with me, Lord." The approval of a great host of people was no substitute for that friendship. Solomon would one day ask for wisdom, and the request would please God. Moses asked for a companion, one that would never leave his side, would lead and guide every step, would make life's bitter moments sweet and give warmth and intimacy to the lonely hours. It was exactly what he needed and God honored the plea, even as He would Solomon's.

It's been suggested that Moses must have been bitterly disappointed that he was denied entrance to the land which had been his goal for so many years. It's much more likely that by now God's friendship had become far more tangible a reality than the land of milk and honey. Wherever God was, *that* was where he wanted to be. With eye undimmed and step as firm as ever, he turned his face toward Mt. Nebo—alone. Slowly he climbed toward its rocky summit. Below him, on the plain, the evening campfires were being lit. Had the people forgotten him already? Were they thinking of tomorrow and the next day and the next —the glorious culmination of this wretched forty years? It didn't matter.

He turned his eyes westward where, in the light of the setting sun, lay Canaan. It had no special charm for him now. God was as surely with him here as He would be with His people. The message had been the same for both: "Be strong and of good courage, do not fear or be in dread . . . for it is the Lord . . . who goes with you; he will not fail you or forsake you." For Moses the added dimension that took from this last mountain-top experience its bitterness was the relationship with a friend, One who called him intimately by name and spoke to him face-to-face. What more could a triumphal entry into Canaan ever offer him than that?

5

Lonely Hero

"I can't believe this guy. I mean—he gives me goose bumps!"

"Yeh, I know what you mean. Wow, what a build! And the way he looks at you. . . ."

"*If* you're pretty."

"There you go again. Sour grapes. Just because he's never looked in *your* direction. . . ."

"I don't see him looking in yours either. I'd think he'd have more important things to do, anyway . . . after all . . . a man of God and everything."

The three friends eyed each other uncomfortably. The conversation hadn't gone quite the way any of them had intended. Even if they weren't exactly superspiritual, they did belong to the "people of God." Whatever that meant. And this fellow— he was something else. Who could deny it? They let loose in another rhapsody.

"His muscles . . . wow!"

"The way he walks. . . ."

"The zany things he does. . . ."

Israel's brightest hope of deliverance was being verbally tossed back and forth like the local *enfant terrible* usually is. And he couldn't care less. Long ago he'd written off the local girls. Maudlin bunch. No class. Too available. The guys were just as bad. Besides, he had this special mission. It was exciting to know that God had put His finger on him to deliver a whole nation from under the Philistine heel. He'd do it too—without any help. And he'd have a whale of a time doing it.

Samson wasn't in error when it came to the sense of destiny that drove him. He was cut out to be a hero, equipped from birth for a special mission. It had taken a miracle to make fruitful the barren womb from which he came. In a way it reflected the larger barrenness of the whole nation. There didn't seem to be an energizing spark anywhere on the scene to touch off a regenerative impulse, any more than the sad farmwife of Zorah had hope of a son.

When that miracle did happen it hinged on something that reaches down through the ages to touch us in the twentieth century—the vow of separation. It had taken effect before ever Samson was born. No wine to set the spirit tingling and release the inhibitions. The godly mother had no problem there. Neither was she to touch anything unclean. As good as done. Happily the promise was made that young Samson's life would bear the same marks of separation. The pains of birth were forgotten when she saw the proud father holding his lusty son in his arms. Perfect.

Not quite. A certain tendency showed itself from the cradle. He was a feisty one, this child. His doting father hardly knew whether to be amused or worried. He had a temper, but then righteous indignation was a good trait to develop for the job at hand. He was impatient of help, but the times required a man that could stand alone. He didn't take advice readily, but then who needed it if God spoke directly to His servant? In all these things the aged father could comfort himself. Anyway, Samson's name suited him well. *Sunny* was the Hebrew translation. *Irrepressible* was perhaps more like it. Who could deny anything to a cute little fellow like him?

It was when he began making decisions of his own that all the traits intensified. An ungovernable temper wasn't quite the same thing as a sunny disposition. And the self-denial that the parents had practiced didn't automatically transfer to young Samson. The heedless *joie de vivre* that the forbidden wine symbolized was his passion, and the spirit of independency that the razor stood for was equally his. As for partaking of things unclean, his spirit seemed to crave the most spiritually debilitating sensual pleasures. All the outward symbolism he adhered to so religiously was flagrantly denied by his way of life. That it all came off with a certain *élan* pulled the wool over Dad's eyes and made him a hero to his peers. This then was Israel's bright hope. Was it really the best that God could find? It hardly seemed possible.

Samson, like every child, held the promise of a new beginning for his family, for his nation. The wretched history of Israel could have been turned around by one committed person, but the separation from sin that God required had to be his own— not merely a promise made by grateful parents. God's promise for Abraham had been built upon a premise: "For I know him, that he will command his children and his household after him, and they shall keep the way of the LORD, to do justice and judgment; that the Lord may bring upon Abraham that which he hath spoken of him" (Genesis 18:19). Unfortunately, Samson seemed pretty much of a freewheeler in his own home.

Samson's dad was so preoccupied with the mechanics of the Nazarite vow that he forgot that the outward conformity to its precepts was to be a reflection of an inner commitment. Samson was the P. K. (Preacher's Kid) of his day—whose parents dedicate him body and soul in sincerest fervor to the Lord's work before ever he's born—and then leave him behind as they piously pursue their high calling. His parents were so thrilled at having a miracle son—and what a son—that they developed a huge blind spot, big enough to cover the spectacle Sam was making of himself without their ever noticing. They carefully observed the negative aspects of the Nazarite's vow but forgot the positive. And what they forgot, Samson had apparently never experienced—that separation is not only *from* sin but *unto* God. This is where it all went wrong for young Sam. Unwilling to walk *alone* with God, and finding fault with God's people, he sought his companionship with the enemy—the exciting, provocative enemy—and that was his downfall.

The times demanded an intrepid leader—one that was fearless, bold, decisive, as wily as his adversaries. Samson was all of these. Certainly the blood coursed hot and vigorously in his veins, generating tremendous energy that God could have used in His plan if only Samson had been willing to be controlled by the Holy Spirit. Too late he would discover that God knew best. God called Samson in all the vigor of his young manhood to place himself and all of his talents at His disposal. He was no Jeremiah, and God didn't intend him to be. Not for him the thirty years as a lonely figure calling down doom from the temple steps on an unrepentant people. Neither was he to be a solitary voice crying in the wilderness as was John. Sociable Sam would never have made that scene. Moses could live in the desert for forty years and be content. Elijah lived by the brook of Cherith without complaint until he was ordered to move on. Either situation would have been a trial greater than convivial Samson could have borne.

On the contrary, a wise God called a talented and engaging young man—not quite the stereotype of the biblical prophet—to judge Israel and deliver her from Philistine oppression. Conformity to Christ's image doesn't obliterate one's own personality—but it *does* require a submission that Samson's independent spirit was unwilling to give even to the God of Israel. He liked the idea of being Israel's deliverer, but wanted to do it his own way—and above all his mission must not interfere with the wayward life he loved.

A whole generation of Israel's youth had already suffered for the somnambulism of the nation. Certainly it wasn't revival time when the young Samson strode through the streets of Zorah, turning the girls' heads and arousing jealousy in the lads. To have everything the young people admired plus the special calling of God put him in a class by himself already. He had so much going for him that by contrast the kids in the local youth group seemed like louts and bores. We've all known Samsons in our churches. They seem carried along effortlessly by a certain charisma that neither art nor effort can imitate. One can't doubt that the hand of God has touched them in a special way. But, as with Samson, a certain feeling of immunity from the checks and balances of a corporate Christian life creeps in and even the laudable desire to do great things in the name of the Lord draws the Samsons into a place of spiritual isolation and potential danger. Being so much more talented than anyone else, there is no one from whom they are willing to take advice—and being out of touch with their brethren inevitably cuts them off from God.

Being in a class by oneself can be a lonely position. The hero whose name is on every lip and who is mobbed and cheered wherever he goes is usually one of the loneliest people in the world. Everyone knows his name and his accomplishments, but no one knows *him.* Nor does he often know himself. God never intended for any of us to be idolized. The worshiping fans forget that the great quarterback, MVP of the latest Super Bowl, is just a human being, and the Academy Award-winning actress is really made of the same stuff as the rest of us. Hero worship sets a human being on a pedestal of isolation and loneliness that has brought many to suicide at the height of a "successful career" that apparently did not satisfy their real needs as human beings. Beneath the bulging muscles and bravado, Samson was a lonely man craving for genuine love and companionship. Unfortunately for him and for Israel, he sought it in illicit sex and sensuality—and anyone who had listened with even half an ear to the voice of God could have predicted the tragic outcome.

Individualism has characterized the philosophy of our own youth culture of the past two decades, deceiving and destroying multitudes with its false promise of so-called freedom that in the end turns out to be slavery to drugs, sex, and peer pressure. How strange it is that in the name of "non-conformity" everyone begins to look exactly alike and to behave exactly alike, from clothes to hair-styles to music to life-style. Following the recently popular slogan, "Do your *own* thing," millions apparently failed to realize that they were all doing the *same* thing. The selfish motivation of the hippie culture has spilled over into every segment of society, with women, children, the aged, criminals, the professions, homosexuals—in a word, just about everybody—demanding their untrammeled freedom. But no society can survive without some restrictions on behavior. The paradise Haight Ashbury was intended to be turned into hell, because there were no guidelines as everyone did his thing. The line must be drawn somewhere—but where? Modern youth is returning to this question after throwing it out for two decades. If we do not draw the line where God draws it, then we are left with the majority vote, opposed by the cry for minority rights, and the changing tastes and fashions of society which only confuse and can never satisfy—because they have no moral basis. Man created in the image of God really craves divine guidance, in spite of all the bluster about independence. A generation of idealists floundering without an ideal has demonstrated the tragic consequences of rejecting absolutes. Centuries earlier Samson had already discovered the same truth—but unfortunately only when it was too late to repair his shattered life. Perhaps we can learn from his mistakes and save ourselves from the same disaster.

Predictably Mom and Dad panicked when Sam started going to Timnath. "So what's in Timnath that we haven't got here, son?" came the feeble question, instead of the resounding rebuke he needed.

"Cool it, Dad. I'm just making the scene. After all, you've got to know your enemy."

"That well, Sam?"

"You're talking about this girl? Don't worry. I won't get involved. It's just that these local chicks give me a pain."

"But, son. . . ."

Already Samson was out the door, leaving Mom and Dad looking at each other in helpless bewilderment. It wasn't far to Timnath, with its vineyards and olive groves and cornfields. It should have belonged to the Israelites, but instead its inhabitants were constantly harassing the people of Dan who occupied her borders. It was downright embarrassing, this growing camaraderie with the enemy. Worse yet, it was getting harder and harder to explain it all to the youth leader at the local Shabbat school. A terrible reflection on *them*. That hurt most of all.

"Wife, we must do something."

"You're the head of the house. So do it."

"But you're the one the angel spoke to way back there. What was it he said about bringing up Sam? Where have we gone wrong?"

"You've got me. I haven't taken a drop since that day, and I keep a kosher table. It's a total mystery!"

Like Eli, Samson's parents seemed to hide their eyes from what was really happening. Without parental restraint, all of their prayers and dedication were not enough to put the brakes on his self-will and waywardness. He didn't seem abashed to hurry home with the news that he'd found a girl friend in Timnath. "Get her for me." The twice reiterated demand seemed to imply a certain confidence that they'd comply. Indeed, on his next visit Mom and Dad themselves came along. Though it was a flagrant violation of God's laws—and doubly so for a Nazarite—in apparent approval they participated at the wedding feast. Samson must have thought it a sufficient argument that he couldn't divulge the riddle to his new wife because he hadn't yet told it to Mom and Dad. And finally, when the wedding shambles was at last over, it was back to his parents' home that Samson skulked. Yes, many a twentieth-century parent would envy Samson's mother and father for the way their boy stuck around home—between excursions anyway. Sam was a lad who needed all the help he could get, but despite all of his exposure he certainly wasn't getting it at home.

He wasn't getting it from the Zorah crowd either. Feebly as he had expressed it, Dad was right when he asked whether there wasn't some local girl that Samson could feel compatible with. Like many a church today, perhaps there wasn't much about the local congregation that inspired or attracted young Sam. Nothing to "draw the young people." But there must have been a few earnest young seekers after God even in that colorless little town of Zorah—and some that would have responded to his example. Samson needed them—desperately. And they needed him. But somehow they went their separate ways, never quite getting together. Wholesome relationships with others tend to encourage right inhibitions, the kind that provide the checks to impulsive or irresponsible behavior and allow the individual to see himself in the right perspective. Samson deprived himself of this deterrent, and with a personality like his —it was disastrous.

Of course Samson, as a God-appointed deliverer, had been given all he needed to do the job. It took strength. He had it. It took courage. He had plenty. It took divine inspiration. It was available. But, with no rule over his own spirit, Samson was like a city whose walls are broken down. The fact that he *could* carry Gaza's gates into the desert proved his strength; that this is *how* he expended his God-given energy proved how little control he did have over his impulses.

Like all of us, Samson badly needed to share himself, to give voice to his real feelings and aspirations; in honest humility to admit his fears and failings, and in intimate fellowship with even one other like-minded person to pray about all the things that concerned him and his nation. To a large extent, it was his own pride and pretense to self-sufficiency that forged the loneliness he suffered from. He might have tried to blame others for not being sympathetic and understanding, for not reaching out to him—but that only blinded him to his own unapproachableness. He hadn't given the right people a chance, and his rejection of them had driven him to seek solace from the enemies of God. That could only lead to his undoing.

In large part it was his own image of himself as a national hero that doomed him to the lonely isolation that eventually destroyed him. He couldn't be himself and come down to the level of honestly sharing life with just plain people. It had to be someone with "class" like Delilah. Samson had become so dependent upon that mistaken image of himself that when his locks were at last shorn on Delilah's knees he was totally unaware that God had departed from him. The self-sufficiency that others had envied in Samson was his Achilles' heel, because it robbed him of the real sufficiency that is only found in God and without which even a he-man hero cannot survive.

Psychologists tell us that show-offs are usually insecure and lonely people. The painfully shy react in the same exaggerated way. In my own experience, the agonies of walking down the main aisle of a crowded high-school cafeteria came out in a certain air of hauteur, totally unrelated to the misery felt inside. Samson's antics were a covering of a different kind but equally devastating, for there were probably enough characters in Zorah like the charmers on our opening page for Samson to feel compelled to keep up the image. He had the audience but not the cast, and was definitely not in touch with the Director, which made center stage a lonely spot.

Samson wasn't by any stretch of the imagination an adolescent— except in behavior—when he sent the foxes, tail to burning tail, among the Philistines' corn, but like a teenager fearful of being a nobody, he set out to prove himself. In no way was Samson about to be forgotten. By no one. Anywhere. The skittering foxes, the city gates carried into the desert, the teasing repartee on Delilah's knees—all highlighted an actor without a director—literally. That magnificent body wasn't in subjection to its divine Head, and the resulting spectacle must have grieved the Danites as much as it infuriated the Philistines. It's said that a child needs love most when he least deserves it. Certainly Samson needed not only a restraining God-relationship but a healthy interchange with his own people. It's also true that it's better to be alone than in bad company. He thought he had found some friends to ease the loneliness—but they were the wrong kind, thoroughly false beneath their smiling facades, and the very enemy he should have been subduing.

For how many young people has the creeping spiritual paralysis in their own lives begun with the wrong friend! The young man or woman, boy or girl, cannot exist without friends to share with, to let off steam with. No doubt Samson told himself very sincerely before he first went down to Timnath that he needed "to have a friend *somewhere.*" The first step down is usually a rationalization. His mission was a double one: to quell the enemy and to judge his own people. When once they had discovered his pitiful moral weakness, the enemy laughed at poor Samson behind his back. Without obedience to God—no matter how invincible physically—he was powerless over the enemy and unable to exercise the right influence over his own people. His testimony should have been solidly established in Israel first—even as ours should be—in our homes, our churches, our neighborhoods, our schools.

True, the Spirit of the Lord came "at times" upon Samson on his own turf, but his hit-and-run testimony could scarcely compensate for the rest. The mind remained unclouded by strong drink and the hair hung unshorn as ever, but what Samson was and did spoke far more loudly than his mechanical observance of Nazaritism. When a man of God goes bad the world is outraged as it never is against the casual and habitual sinner.

Despite the escapades, Samson went unscathed, in one scrape and out another. There was one area, however, in which everything went wrong—his love life—and that's where the bitter has mingled with the sweet for many a Christian leader. Otherwise wholly the intrepid hero, wanting no help, needing no help, here Samson came totally unglued. "My son, give *me* thy heart . . . keep thy heart with all diligence, for out of it are the issues of life . . . thou shalt love the Lord thy God with all thy heart and with all thy mind and with all thy strength." There isn't much interpretation possible here. Again it's fellowship *with* as well as separation *from.* Samson had given his heart to an enemy of God and of His people. Who could be so blind as not to see what the inevitable outcome would be?

I remember so well the young Rumanian student who approached my car in the twilight as I was parked in the streets of his city one evening in 1974. There was a furtive look around, followed by some posed questions, and then a floodgate of pent-up rage was unloosed as he whispered his complaints. There was no one among family and friends that he could trust, no one he could talk to freely about his deepest feelings and aspirations. It was impossible to form genuine friendships in the police state in which he lived. He'd clutched at me, a stranger, in order to give vent to his frustration. When in the next moments a bystander seized him and ordered him off, I sensed a little of what he must have felt. With this lad the isolation wasn't voluntary. Far from it. For Samson it was. He'd made a choice, and we can only be surprised that *he* seemed surprised at the outcome.

How often Samson must have walked down the path that traversed the no-man's land between his two worlds. Back and forth he went, never really belonging in either environment. Too much an Israelite to be comfortable in Philistia, he was at the same time too much a worldling to be happy among his own people. The inner conflict dulled the pleasures to be found in Gaza and made miserable interludes of his visits home. On occasion God was causing the wrath of man to praise Him in spite of Samson. We're told he *began* to deliver Israel. But he was like a runner who had deliberately shackled himself with every conceivable hindrance to a successful race. Certainly he was running with the wrong team. It's never the aim of the non-Christian to strengthen the believer. The rewards for betraying Samson were far greater for Delilah than the rewards of faithfulness. All her energies were directed toward finding his one vulnerable spot and she did find it—like the professional she was.

Blinded and condemned to grind in an underground Philistine prison, Samson finally caught sight of his mission. Unable now to seek solace for his lonely heart in any other direction, he looked up in desperation to the God of Israel who had been waiting all this time to be his Friend. Faced by reality as he'd never allowed himself to be before, fun-loving, convivial Samson became a Nazarite in heart at last. Never would he see his aged parents or his long-suffering people again. The last time they'd met had been on top of the rock of Elam. The men of Dan had chided him then for exposing the tribe needlessly to the Philistines' ire. His answer had been, as expected, "I did them like they did me." It seemed a sufficient reason.

Thereafter it was mutual treachery on all fronts until the day Samson stood sightless between the pillars of a heathen temple. This time the entertainment was at his expense. The once-lustful eyes were darkened, the wayward feet shackled: but again in grace God's Spirit moved mightily on his unprofitable servant and Samson had a final lonely victory. Instead of the beautiful living sacrifice that God wants us to present in fellowship with our brothers and sisters, the best he could do was to offer his dead body. Little good that errant flesh had done in life. It was only slightly more useful in death.

6

"Call Me Mara"

At the crossroads the three women were having a good cry. They had reason to cry, no doubt about that. There wasn't much more these three could lose and still come out of it in one piece. The older one especially. A widow at an age when she'd have no chance of remarrying, Naomi had also lost the two sons who could have supported her in her old age. And that wasn't all! She was on her way back to Bethlehem after a ten-year parenthesis in the land of Moab, where her family had gone years before to escape a Judean famine. That was where one disaster after another had shattered her life. Now it was empty-handed back to the old hometown to explain it all to the folks there. That wasn't going to be easy either. Bitterly she wept—long and loud.

Today, some three thousand years later, she would have plenty of company, with more than one out of three once-married women widowed or divorced, and an increasing percentage either choosing or being compelled by circumstances to make a go of it on their own. Despite the long way baby is supposed to have come since the days of her chores-children-church-enclosed world, most women still relate their happiness quotient to whether or not there's a man in their lives. We try in a hundred ways to conceal the emptiness, but there it is—

that feeling of dependence on an arm stronger than ours and the need for an intimate sharing that seems possible only to those who have been made one flesh.

It's the emotional dependence that's lingered long after Eve was presented as a gift to Adam. A woman wants to feel cherished. There's no substitute for that delicious sense of being desirable, intriguing, indispensable. Neither can anything replace a love that's kind and patient and suffers long, a love that covers a multitude of sins. Naomi must have had this kind of relationship to miss Elimelech so much. A husband—or the lack of one—was uppermost in her thinking, always. A prominent psychologist has declared that half of his women patients come to him because they're married and the other half because they're not. For Naomi marriage was obviously the focal point of her existence.

Of course, like most of us, Naomi probably had her off days when she secretly wished that her Elimelech would just go away on a business trip for a few days . . . a fishing jaunt . . . anything, so she could be alone for a change. The time did come for her —with a vengeance—and she learned what it was to step across the threshold of an empty house. She knew the cold comfort of an empty bed and the silence of a table set for one. The knowledge that the doorbell won't ring at six, nor will anyone answer to one's own knock or call makes terribly real the truth of what God did when He made two *one* flesh. The separation truly is a cutting asunder and it hurts. The future—uncertain and frightening as old age approaches—must now be faced alone.

Whatever the emotional vacuum left by Naomi's loss, the material one was bad enough. No Social Security checks to count on, no tax breaks, widow's pension, mortgage insurance, half-fares, or food stamps. There was no way of earning a living. All Naomi could hope for was charity. She'd lost a lot and she knew it.

Yes, Naomi cried at the crossroads. Thousands of women are crying at that same crossroads today, and crying so loudly that they overlook some of the beautiful solutions that God has placed at their very elbows. For Naomi that key was her daughter-in-law and the way she worked out her own loss. We often forget that these two women were both widows, but so differently did they handle their grief that the one stands out as the very epitome of hopeless sorrow and the other as a ray of comforting sunshine in her mother-in-law's embittered heart.

Certainly Elimelech hadn't brought his family to Moab with any thought of either of his boys marrying one of the despised Moabite girls. Before ever the Israelites had entered the land of Canaan, these seductive women had caused many of their young soldiers to sin and even to sacrifice to strange gods. What an embarrassment his sons' marriages must have been to good, upright Elimelech and his faithful wife, though we know they must have tried to make the best of it. Ruth's and Orpah's loyalty bear that out.

Added to that disappointment there must have been the nagging realization that they weren't experiencing God's best in their lives, either as a family or as a nation. What could you expect, with men like Samson judging the land? The spiritual emptiness gnawed at the moral fiber of the nation just as surely as hunger gnawed at the stomach. The children of Israel were designed with a built-in God-shaped vacuum and only rarely was it being filled in those days. Little wonder there was a famine.

The separations we experience aren't always God's best either. We know that. The death of a beloved husband or divorce from an incompatible one inflicts wounds that our loving Father finds no delight in, but which He can use to make the fabric of our lives work together for good. How do we accept those wounds? With no real hope for a better life, Ruth went, nevertheless, with serenity and with determination. What a beautiful combination—the sweet and loving disposition and at the same time this gut-level moral and physical energy. "Where *you* go, I will go. Don't try to change my mind on that. Your God will be *my* God. My decision's made. Your people *will* be my people. I'll win them over, somehow. I know I will, with God's help."

With all the good resolves made and voiced and sealed with action, Ruth faced the future. And there's the key—that expectation that the future will not be as the past has been. "Hope is . . . perhaps, the chief happiness which this world affords," said Samuel Johnson. "Everything that is done in the world is done by hope," echoed Martin Luther King in a later age. For the Christian there's the added dimension of a hope that "maketh not ashamed"—or never disappoints (Romans 5:5). To the assurance of God's love and faithfulness Ruth added the willing heart that lends hands and feet to His promises.

"You can't go home again," Thomas Wolfe tells us. The joys of the past can never be re-created. We idealize that perfect vacation in Hawaii and scrimp and save and, delirium of joy, ten years later we go again—and are terribly disappointed. How Hawaii has changed! No. We've changed. A happy experience is unique and it's creative. Part of ourselves is absorbed into that moment or day or special year, never to be recycled. But the beauty of it is that *new* joys and experiences are forever germinating, ready to nudge their way into existence. All they need is to be nurtured and cultivated and coaxed into the sunlight.

But Naomi lingered over the past bitterness as she placed one weary foot after the other. And how contagious her recital at the crossroads was. "God is against me. Turn back."

(But Naomi, God is faithful after all. Don't you see your daughter-in-law by your side? Open your eyes. Don't be blind like Elisha's servant. There are invisible chariots of fire surrounding you now, holding back the oppressive power of Satan.)

"See, Orpah has left. Run along after your sister-in-law, Ruth. I'll be *(sob)* all right."

No way was Ruth going to run along, but so wrapped up was

Naomi in the total hopelessness of her situation that she gave up arguing at last. What a stubborn girl this Ruth was. Silently the two turned their faces toward Bethlehem and trudged on.

As with so many who face deep and sustained sorrow, Naomi's feeling of self-esteem had suffered. She couldn't imagine that either of her two daughters-in-law really *wanted* to remain with her, even though it must have been her godly life that had won them from their own heathen worship, and there must have been endearing qualities that had won this loyalty to her personally. Ruth had dealt kindly with her and her dead sons. She witnessed to that. But to leave home and loved ones and country to accompany their destitute mother-in-law to a strange land? It hardly seemed possible that Ruth would sacrifice so much for so little.

What a sensation their arrival in Bethlehem caused.

"That woman over there . . . can it be . . . Naomi? What a change!"

"It's obvious . . . some tragedy—but look, the young woman with her. I've never seen *her* before."

"You don't suppose she's one of those *Moabite* girls . . . you know . . . married her son?"

The momentary disapproval disintegrated in hugs and tears as the old friends fell on each other's necks.

"Don't call me Naomi, girls. Call me Mara. The Lord has really been hard on me." *And will no doubt continue to be,* her tone must have implied.

How often when sorrow comes into our lives, our hearts, if not our lips, accuse God as Naomi did. "The Almighty hath afflicted me." After all, He could have prevented it if He'd *wanted* to. He didn't want to, so there must be some defect in His love. It was hardly the way Joseph interpreted his misfortunes. Thrown into a pit, sold to slave traders, falsely accused, cast into prison and elevated at last to the second place in Pharaoh's kingdom, he disarmed the brothers who'd started it all with the gracious words, "You meant it for evil, but the Lord meant it for good." Joseph's cross was cruelty and injustice. Ruth's and Naomi's was the loss of home and husband and children. In both cases the Master Designer was weaving a beautiful pattern which, from the perspective of either prison or graveside, was totally unrecognizable. Like Joseph, Ruth faced the dark places with serenity and determination.

The babble of voices rose and fell in the dusty streets of Bethlehem, and all the while Ruth waited in her mother-in-law's shadow, eyes downcast, feeling the appraising glances, sensing the veiled implication that all the bad things that had happened to Naomi in her homeland had somehow left their stigma on *her*. Unflinchingly she stood there and reminded herself of her resolve: These people *would* become her people.

What a treasure Naomi had brought with her in this simple, unprepossessing Moabite girl. She was apparently totally overlooked in all of Naomi's thinking. There was love, yes, and gratitude. There must have been some sort of introduction to the townsfolk who gathered that day. "Oh, by the way, this is Ruth, my beloved Chilion's widow. She's been good to me. Receive her for my sake." But Ruth in no way figured in her thoughts of the future. In Naomi's thinking, she'd come home alone, yet all the while the key to a new life had plodded faithfully at her side. She'd come home *empty*, as she had said, but it was at the time of barley harvest. She should have known that no needy one ever remained destitute then. But so great was the grief that as far as Naomi was concerned, the picture couldn't have been blacker.

Of course Naomi had cause to weep. Jesus Himself wept. Paul reminds us that we do sorrow, but not "as others which have no hope" (I Thessalonians 4:13). For Naomi the tears came for the wrong reasons. In fact, she cried the hardest when she was at the entrance to the very village that Micah prophesied would be the birthplace of the Messiah. The immensity of what God was doing through the badly underrated girl at her side passed her completely by, and she stood dissolved in tears on the threshold of a new life.

We've all experienced the forelorn feeling of being alone in our sorrow—and found later that God was nearer than we ever suspected. "My God, my God, why hast thou forsaken me?" (Psalms 22:1) cried David in one breath, and with the next, "I will fear no evil, for thou art with me . . ." (22:4). The anguish was real. No one could have convinced David otherwise at the moment, but when the pain was over and the healing had come, he would have been the first to testify that God had been there all the time.

It's the nature of loneliness—this distorted view, or rather this blindness. One wonders if Naomi ever did anything but enumerate her miseries to her long-suffering companion on the weary journey back to Bethlehem. The home she'd once had, the ease, the honor, the good husband, fine sons, and, finally, every detail of the latters' lives from the first tooth to final illness. Indeed, for all Naomi knew, she did return empty —empty of all but memories. Resigned to a life of loneliness from now on, she had begun to cling to her sorrow as though *that* gave her some status—at least it was a ready topic of conversation that she could belabor again and again.

Are we ever so preoccupied with our grief and loneliness that we don't recognize the Ruths at our sides? Perhaps she's there in very unprepossessing form—someone we may have never valued when things went well with us. God has His ministering spirits where we least expect to find them, even where we *can't* find them, and we learn only later that our lives have been touched by one of these "angels unawares."

Even as the lonely often fail to recognize the help at hand, so they fail to recognize their own inner resources. Naomi had surrendered her own self-esteem as though that were a necessary consequence of the loss of husband, sons, and possessions. Feeling worthy neither of God's intervening kindness nor of her daughter-in-law's love, how could she have a sense of self-worth? Surely she'd hit an all-time low in the art of self-isolation. This can become a habit, an automatic reflex in defeat, yet it is a form of pride in reverse. Afraid to fight back in the face of tragedy for fear of losing again, we adopt the ultimate excuse for ourselves by blaming it all on "the way the ball bounces." There's no use trying because *"nothing* ever works out right for *me* anyway." Naomi had reached this point. "Call me Mara— the Lord has dealt bitterly with me. It's not *my* fault . . . and of course I can't fight *Him,* so . . . what's the use?"

And Ruth. Her very name means *friend of God.* Who could be totally desolate with such a friend? That He was a comparatively new friend, too, was perhaps to her advantage. The freshness of first encounter was still there. It's often the new Christian who copes best with trial. There's that simple expectancy that God can and will surely do what is needful, since He has just demonstrated His great power in the miracle of new birth. To the newly converted nothing seems too hard. This beautiful relationship with Naomi's God had relieved the bitterness of loss for Ruth, had eased the weary journey for her, and now would see her through the difficult period of adjustment to a new home and people. Instead of coming back feeling empty, Ruth walked into the town of Bethlehem in company with an invincible Friend.

The bereaved young widow was rich in other ways. In a culture where women rarely moved beyond the sheltering framework of home and family and local friendships, Ruth wasn't afraid to step out of the old context and try something new. That it was with Naomi's God that she went mitigated the terror, but it was a very big step, nevertheless, that Ruth took when she turned her back on all that was familiar. Fear can be the paralyzing factor that locks the lonely forever within a sterile life pattern. Fierce loyalty to a place—or a memory— isn't always God's perfect way. Sometimes economic necessity will even force one into a new realm of life that would never have been attempted otherwise. With Ruth it was a matter of choice, which makes her doubly admirable.

The two women had arrived at Bethlehem just at barley harvest. It couldn't have taken Ruth long to put this fact to work for her and her mother-in-law. Food they needed. Nothing debatable about that. And with energy and enthusiasm Ruth headed for the likeliest field to glean. It highlights another characteristic of this unusual young woman: the ability to recognize opportunity when it came knocking. Certainly those waiting handfuls didn't require any great talent to gather. They were just *there,* for the taking, by whoever had the gumption to go and get them. The choice was hers. Either she could stay home and lament, or she could go and help herself. All the handfuls in the world left on purpose by a generous Boaz wouldn't have done her any good if she hadn't recognized the opportunity available in the neighboring fields.

Ruth didn't underestimate her resources. It was a quality that contrasted with the sense of worthlessness that left her mother-in-law prostrated. Early in her spiritual experience Ruth was learning that it was possible to be "troubled on every side, yet not distressed; . . . perplexed, but not in despair; Persecuted, but not forsaken; cast down, but not destroyed" (2 Corinthians 4:8, 9). She learned the reassuring fact that God supplies according to the *need.* A healthy young body Ruth had. Add to that that it was barley harvest. No need for Elijah's ravens to feed these two. Action was part of God's healing therapy and Ruth pitched in with a will.

Even old Naomi wasn't as empty as she imagined. She carried something back to Bethlehem which she could never lose, and it was her unique contribution to this winning combination. No one who keeps an unblemished good name as Naomi had goes empty-handed. She had given that name by way of marriage to Ruth, and without it Ruth would never have won her husband or her place in history. So, each in her own way, contributed her part to the working of God's plan.

The lonely and bereaved often don't have the courage or emotional reserves to plan intelligently for the future. The best they can manage is a day-by-day acceptance of the way that they must go. When Ruth woke up that first morning in a strange town, she wasn't faced with the next 365 friendless and hungry days all at once. There was no way that that first dawn could cancel out the rancor of generations or ten years of poverty. On the contrary, it was the necessities of *that day* she faced. It meant recognizing that day's need for food and deliberately turning her feet in the direction of the ripe fields. It meant gathering sufficient for one day and all the while facing with gracious mien the speculative glances of her fellow workers. The next day she set out again to gather for that day's need. Sandall's beautiful hymn expresses it so well.

> Day by day and with each passing moment,
> Strength I find to meet my trials here;
> Trusting in my Father's wise bestowment,
> I've no cause for worry or for fear.
>
> He whose heart is kind beyond all measure
> Gives unto each day what He deems best—
> Lovingly, its part of pain and pleasure,
> Mingling toil with peace and rest.

Because Ruth wasn't unrealistically ambitious or demanding, there was no chance to be disappointed. Having come to Bethlehem materially "empty," there was no way to go but up anyway. It wasn't by any means an attitude that negated the hope that tomorrow would be better, only that today could be coped with if taken a moment at a time. Surely Ruth's hope wasn't in her circumstances anyway. There wasn't any earthly reason that she knew of that those would ever change. But she had reason to hope in the God of Israel. "Why art thou cast down, O my soul?" David asked himself. ". . . Hope thou in God" (Psalms 42:5). And with this healthy, happy hope before her, Ruth gleaned each day's blessing in the fields of Boaz.

Ruth had learned another secret that drives away the loneliness, though she was likely too guileless ever to think of it as a virtue. It wasn't primarily to fill her own need that she labored daily under the hot sun. Lonely and destitute as she was, there was one whose pain was greater than hers. At least it seemed so in her self-effacing eyes. Naomi had drawn her loneliness around her like a shroud and topped it off with a label for all of Bethlehem to take note of. That new name *Mara* said it all, and with compassion Ruth poured herself out for the sake of her grieving mother-in-law. How much of Ruth's own anguish must have been lightened in that sacrificial service. "Seldom can a heart be lonely if it seeks a lonelier still/Self-forgetting, seeking only emptier cups to fill." Frances Ridley Havergal knew intense suffering herself, but her poems fall like sunshine on dark places because they reflect a self-forgetting concern for *others*.

There's no evidence that the garrulous women who so eagerly crowded around their returning friend participated in her healing. They lent willing ears. No doubt they came on strong with an "Oh, dear!" and "What a pity!" and a "You don't say," but it takes more than curiosity or even commiseration to prove that one really cares. Ruth gave this added dimension.

Cherished, cared for, nurtured at last, Naomi began to experience a healing in her own spirit on the day that Ruth returned to relate her experience in the field of Boaz. From that moment on, her every utterance was one of hope. It was "Blessed be [Boaz] of the Lord," and "It is *good* my daughter . . ." and "Shall I not seek rest for thee, that it may be well with thee?" From despair to hope to the feeling that nothing was impossible! It was quite a trip for Naomi, and she would have missed it entirely if it hadn't been for simple, unassuming, loving Ruth.

It could have all turned out so differently. What did Ruth really have except her own inner resources and a great God? And what she *was* had so quickly been gossiped from mouth to mouth, that when she confronted Boaz on that first day of work he knew all about her already. Beautiful. News of the loving care she'd lavished on Naomi had preceded her to his field. Boaz knew that she'd left father and mother for Naomi's sake. He was fully aware that she'd elected to take up life among strangers, a uniquely frightening experience for a young woman of those times. "Let the Lord pay you back and give you a full reward!" How beautiful those words must have sounded to Ruth, and yet she turned them into a compliment for Boaz. "Let me find favor in your eyes. You've comforted me by speaking in so friendly a way to me, even though I'm a stranger." Irresistible Ruth. Who could doubt at this point how the story would end?

Boaz made one more observation before he got down to the business of giving Ruth the specifics on how to make gleaning the best deal in town. He called down a blessing on her from the God of Israel under whose wings she had come to trust. With all the unknowns in her life, Ruth had need of trust, and with all the security of wealth and position that Boaz knew, he still recognized and appreciated that quality. Under those wings there could be no loneliness. Ever the schemer and worrier, Naomi knew that hiding place but hadn't really appropriated it. It wasn't until all the pieces had fallen into place that she could breathe a sigh of relief and relax at last. For Ruth, the wings of Jehovah had become a place of rest before ever she began her labors. Happy, trusting Ruth. In quietness and confidence she'd found her strength.

Barley harvest came and went—and wheat harvest. Every day Ruth turned her feet toward Boaz's fields and bent her back to the work she had to do. No demands on the future. Nightly thanks for the day's mercies. What a life. And still her reputation flourished. "A good name is more to be desired than riches" (Proverbs 22:1). Ruth was fast becoming one of the richest girls in town.

Of course there's more to the story. Ruth continued trusting and Naomi continued scheming. Let's give Naomi the benefit of the doubt and call it *divine* scheming. But the real burden of proof lay with Ruth. That little Moabite stranger who refused to be lonely won over not only Boaz but every last elder in the city gates. The finest wedding congratulation they could think of to bestow on the happy bridegroom was to compare his prize to Rachel and Leah, the mothers of Israel. And the women who'd almost looked through and around and over Ruth when she'd first arrived? For Naomi they could think of no greater blessing when her grandson was laid in her arms than, "Your daughter-in-law who loves you so is better than seven sons."

Ruth was home at last.

7

Asleep at the Post

The old man sat nodding in the sunlight. Against a pillar of the tabernacle he leaned his heavy frame and nodded. Every day for more years than he could remember, life had been the same. From the time of Joshua, Shiloh had been a spiritual center, the people coming and going, with lamb and pigeon and bullock, offering sacrifices to God. Less and less now they needed *him*. His sons had taken over the priestly offices. The thought caused him to stir uneasily. How warm it was. How noisy. More so than usual. An old man needed peace . . . and quiet . . . and sleep. Painstakingly he gathered his robe about him and sank further down into the comforting depths of the soft leather cushion.

Yes, it was busier than usual at Shiloh. For almost a week now the town had been astir with hundreds of visitors who'd come to celebrate the yearly harvest and to commemorate God's covenant made with His people in the Sinai wilderness. Simply constructed palm booths dotted the wayside places, and at night the air was alive with the sound of singing and music and feasting. Soon the excitement would be over for another year and the old priest could nod on undisturbed.

A strange restlessness kept Eli awake. There were so many worshipers pressed within the sacrificial grounds. The air was oppressive with the smell of the blood and smoke that mingled with the swirling dust. Already the crowd was anticipating the evening festivities and hurrying to make their last oblations on the reeking altar.

There was a time when the yearly sacrifice had been alive and vital. It had really meant something. Eli knew it well and the thought disturbed him. The gossip about his sons wasn't *all* deserved, however. It was the types you found here nowadays —hypocrites (out for the excitement), drunken babblers, the women who wouldn't stop at tempting one of God's anointed priests. It was disgusting—the whole scene. That woman over there, for instance, on her knees, swaying, mouthing incoherent words. Drunk—obviously.

For once he spoke out. "Put away your wine, woman!"

Thinking about it later, shame had overwhelmed him. She'd been supplicating God for a son, that was all. How had he mistaken the agonized fervor on that pure face? Was it just so long since someone like her had worshiped at this altar? All he'd been able to say was a hasty, "Go in peace. God grant your request." This woman wanted a son, did she? He knew the feeling well. He'd gotten two. They were even now lurking around the altar somewhere, with fleshhooks—and roving eye. A son, did she say?

With a sigh the old man settled back down into his chair. The sun warmed his back. Ears and eyes grew dull with sleep and again Eli nodded by the temple post.

Eli, asleep at his post already for years, wasn't used to meeting Hannah's type at the temple. He never had too much to say anyway, and before the zeal of this young woman he was more silent than usual. He knew very well why he was there. God had chosen his house to serve Him way back in Egypt. Shiloh was to be a beacon light of testimony throughout Israel and he was to keep the fires burning pure and true and bright. But to confront such a woman as Hannah (who seemed to embody all the qualities he lacked)—the encounter was definitely embarrassing.

What a woman this Hannah was. Nothing weak or uncertain about her. She knew what she wanted and, happily for Israel, what she wanted and what God wanted coincided exactly. It was *she* that asked a son of God. *She* stood up to Eli when she was falsely accused and then graciously covered his embarrassment. *She* decided just when she'd deliver up the child into Eli's care for the temple service. God, husband, priest, and Hannah concurred on each point.

Hers was a very special faith for special circumstances. What mother in her right mind would deliver a young, impressionable child to *that* place? What, after all, were the odds that he would grow up pure and holy and unstained? All Israel despised the two rakes that passed for priests at Shiloh. But it was to the *Lord* she lent the child and not to Eli or even to the Lord's service. Many a parent faces with fear and trepidation the time when eighteen-year-old Sam or Joe or Nan leaves home for college or a job or the service. How will they ever survive away from the protective home environment? Quite simply: they won't—unless they go with a heaven-sent commission—and are themselves in accord with that commission.

Mordecai encouraged Esther with the challenge, "Who knows but that you're come to the kingdom for just such a time as this?" (Esther, chapter 2.) Surrounded by prayer before he was conceived, young Samuel was alert and ready the very first time he heard the voice of God. But it just doesn't work unless both parent and child are agreed. Hannah's assurance that her child was ready for all that Shiloh meant made the lonely home bearable after he was gone. Eli had his children always close at hand and was the lonelier of the two, while Hannah had only a brief, once-a-year reunion with hers. Who could doubt that she felt closer to little Samuel than Eli did to his two sons?

The years passed. Older and more feeble now, Eli lay upon his bed, restless, tormented by the memory of a fearful visitation. To the temple at Shiloh an awesome-visaged prophet had come to tell *him,* Eli, God's anointed-one, the doom that lay over his household. And all because of those high-spirited sons

of his. Nothing specific . . . just the hint in voice and manner
that he should have known what was going on and that it was
serious enough, whatever it was, to merit God's curse. Well
. . . maybe. Boys would be boys. He never could do anything
with them. Just that day he'd tried to speak to them, but how
does one give a fatherly scolding to middle-aged men? Had he
really done all he could when they were young? He wondered.
Now there was this child Samuel in his household, the very
child who'd been the answer to that mother's fervent prayer.
What a comfort he was. With utmost confidence he could leave
the details of the temple service in his small hands. It was a
blessed privilege to have such help when one was old and tired.
He was truly thankful. At last the dull eyes closed. The blessed
drowsiness overcame him and Eli slept.

Not for long. Twice he was awakened out of a deep slumber
by the voice of Samuel at his bedside. "Here I am. You called?"
How quick the child was to do his bidding. Of course he'd been
dreaming and twice he sent him back to bed. A child needed
his sleep, too. The third time Eli came fully awake, and fear
gripped his heart. It must be the voice of God that called the
lad. That voice had been still these many years. Could it be . . . ?

"Samuel, my son, if you hear the voice again, you must
answer, 'Speak, Lord, for thy servant heareth.' "

Trembling, Eli lay his head down once more, following the
quick footfall of the child as he hurried back to do his bidding.

Day dawned, and for once Samuel didn't spring out of bed
and run to open the temple doors and bring Eli his cheerful
morning greeting. Only reluctantly he went, in answer to the
old priest's summons, and reluctantly he told him the terrible
message that confirmed what he already knew. It was no surprise.

"Yes, that's the voice of God. Let Him do what's right," was
all that Eli said before he turned himself to the wall again.

Let's take a closer look at the lonely man who sat so long at
the temple gate, waiting for . . . well, just waiting. It wouldn't

be hard to imagine that post as the starting gate of a race that Eli never quite got into. In fact, he really never even got on his feet. Neither a sitting (nor a lying) position is calculated to inspire action. Kneeling will do, but that requires work—if it's accompanied by prayer. But poor Eli didn't seem well acquainted with that form of exercise either, judging by his treatment of Hannah. Israel's need was so great. It demanded a leader that would strive for the prize of his high calling, one that would run with patience and energy the race that was set before him. Moses had fulfilled his lap when he brought the people to the borders of the Promised Land. Joshua finished his part of the race when he brought them in. Samson, on the other hand, never applied himself to dealing with the enemies that threatened their safety, and Eli never got around to leading the people back to worship, nor did he apparently spend much time at it himself.

Eli was a man singularly without goals or purpose in life. To live without goals is to live without zest or interest. It's a malady peculiar to old age. But shouldn't one relax and reap the rewards of a life of hard work? The answer lies somewhere back in the question. As one was, one will likely continue to be. That Eli didn't know what was going on with his sons except through hearsay comes as no surprise when we realize that neither did he have much discernment of true spirituality when he met it in Hannah. To recognize neither sin nor sanctity leaves Eli with little qualification for his office.

And yet Eli's credentials were just as valid as Samuel's. They were both divinely commissioned. In fact, Eli's household had been set apart in the day of the Pharaohs. What strange lethargy, then, gripped this man? Certainly it wasn't just the natural effects of old age. Despite Browning's cheerful challenge to "Grow old along with me; the best is yet to be," old age is not something most of us look forward to very eagerly. The fear of being alone at that dread time is often more terrifying than the prospect of death itself. David voiced the plaint when he cried out to God, "Cast me not off in the time of old age . . ." (Psalms 71:9). It's that vulnerable time when past joys aren't sufficient to make up for the brief emptiness still ahead.

But for Eli there weren't even memories of a better time. He'd never built for the future. The tremendous opportunities to minister to lives as well as to God when he served at the altar seemingly passed by unnoticed. We're not told how often he took a personal interest in those who came to worship. We only know that the one encounter recorded was a fiasco. Discernment usually goes hand in hand with genuine interest in the individual. We can imagine Eli's uncomfortable feeling that he "really should say something" to the seemingly drunken woman kneeling by the altar. The quick exercise of his priestly "duty" that ensued, however, left Eli floundering in a moment. "Go in peace," he mumbled. It was all the counsel he could summon for the occasion.

Couldn't we say then that one factor in Eli's failure as a priest, a father, and a human being, was his lack of genuine interest in other people? Insights are often intuitive, sometimes cultivated. Lacking the former, Eli never set himself the goal of becoming a perceptive and caring individual. David longed and thirsted after God. He set his heart to pursue good and eschew evil. Despite humiliating failures, he *wanted* very much to excel as a man of God.

Even more tragically, Eli was completely out of it as regards his own family. No doubt things first started going wrong when they were children, but sleepy Eli lacked the energy to cope— even then. It was so much easier to drift, adjust, ignore, delay, anything rather than to be decisive. Being a father takes time and the right usage of time takes self-discipline, and that was definitely not one of Eli's strong points.

The time taken to nourish and support his young lads in their early years would have insured their supportive care and concern—and even their company in his old age. But it was always Samuel who was ready on the instant to answer a call or to fulfill a need. The loving attention from so small a child must have ministered to Eli's lonely spirit, but the contrast with his own wayward and unresponsive sons must have hurt. The one encounter between the three that's recorded wasn't even a dialogue. Eli was very old and in as much of a panic as he'd ever been in, but it was all too late.

"Boys, what's this I hear about your behavior? Everybody's talking."

No answer—naturally. It was a measure of Dad's vital role in the affairs of his children that he had any evidence of their misdeeds only on hearsay. Solomon's admonition to "Correct your son, and he will give you comfort; he will also delight your soul" (Proverbs 29:17) was never intended as a last resort. Never had they seen in their father the example that could have inspired them. Neither very bad nor yet very good, Eli strikes us as a rather ill-defined and corpulent gray area. In a later day Jesus would denounce those like him as fit only to be discarded (Revelation 3:16).

By contrast, the minimal training that Hannah gave young Samuel earned him, as he grew, the favor of both God and men. Even a child is known by his doings, Solomon says in Proverbs 20:11, and the strong-willed mother laid it on the line with hers and then delivered him up totally to the Lord. She must have missed her son. One week during the year wasn't much time to reinforce the relationship, but it was apparently enough. On the other hand, a lifetime within the same sacred temple grounds wasn't enough to acquaint Eli with *his* sons.

Their relationship is reflective of much that passes for family encounter today. More and more youth are on their own in decision-making. Now the new push extends to children, with a vocal organization opting on their behalf for "child power." A major campaign is scarcely needed. The movement's success is assured without the lifting of a finger. Sheer parental inertia, Eli-style, is all that's needed. A child is well able to distinguish between the loneliness of necessity (the deprivation that one is

sometimes called on to suffer for the sake of a higher call) and the loneliness of neglect. Eli was only bearing now what his sons had experienced in their youth. The eager, loving, perhaps a bit anxious eyes that smiled into Samuel's own for such a brief time each fall reminded the young boy that he was infinitely loved and cherished whether present or absent. The little coat that was newly fashioned every year was a daily reminder of that love. Could we dare to imagine that when Hannah returned home, alone, from Shiloh each year she began immediately upon next year's little garment? For both there was a reminder of commitment and the cost of that commitment.

How many missionary parents have agonized over the decision: "Should we or shouldn't we commit ourselves to an isolated post away from Christian friends and all that's socially and morally normal?" How many young people have rebelled at the lack of suitable Christian friends and taken what they could get as some sort of inalienable right to the "pursuit of happiness"? It goes back to the initial commitment, then moves on to consistent communication. Hannah asked for a gift so that she could present that gift back to God. That child became God's responsibility. And she kept her bargain, too. It was *she* who trudged the weary miles to see Samuel every year and to bring him the reminder of her love. This was the communication that kept memory and affection fresh between home and altar. So young—and to be so secure in such an alien place— it must have been the wonder of all Israel.

By contrast, Eli's lethargy cost him not only vital interpersonal relationships with those around him and within his own home, but most of all his aimless existence cost him a relationship with God. "Sweeter as the years go by," the hymn tells us. Not necessarily. Too often old age brings a spiritual relaxation along with the physical lethargy. In Eli's case, it's doubtful the energy had ever been there and old age merely produced in him a caricature of what he'd been when younger.

The need in Israel was so great—and he did nothing. He

apparently felt neither outrage nor urgency at what was going on: the belated scolding he offered his own sons didn't even arouse a response. If there's any doubt that Eli himself was to blame for missing God's call, the denunciation that the child Samuel seconded on that wakeful night must dispel it. His whole house was to be uprooted and destroyed. God couldn't tolerate a man who merely put in time at the temple. Eli may have wept for Israel's tragedy. We're not told. But certain it is that he didn't *do* anything about it.

"If any man *will* come after me, let him deny himself, and take up his cross, and follow me" (Matthew 16:24). Jesus Himself gave the formula for action and it began with a decision, adopting a goal. "My heart is fixed . . ." (Psalms 57:7) David cried out in his zeal to pursue God. Above all, this man wanted his will to be permanently locked into the purposes of God. Significantly, the gravest sin the Bible records of David occurred when, Eli-like, he lounged upon the rooftop when he should have been on the battlefield—and fell to Bathsheba's charms.

One more time we meet Eli, seated by the same temple post where he'd first met the remarkable woman who had asked of God, received, and then given back the son who now provided Israel with the spiritual guidance that his own sons had failed to give. He was waiting anxiously now. Those troublesome warlords from the south, the Philistines, were overrunning the countryside again and had already defeated Israel badly in their first encounter.

There'd been such a clamor at Shiloh—near panic—when the news came. Nobody had consulted *him* when the people demanded that the ark be carried into battle. The Philistines must have known what a holy relic it was. Its very presence would insure success, they cried. And those sons of his had borne it from its resting place and carted it off, to the tumultous acclaim of the rabble crowd. Oh, why hadn't he spoken out? But then, would anyone have listened? "If thou go not with us, carry us not up hence" (*see* Exodus 33:15). Moses had appealed in those words to God before ever he'd set foot on the wilderness journey. The holy ark, with all its reminders of God's deliverance and care, had led their fathers on a forty-year pilgrimage to this land. Would it survive this? Would God be with them this day? There was no voice of inner assurance as Eli sat trembling and waiting for news.

At last the approaching tumult of running feet and despairing cries. Out of his soul's blackness one voice rose above the rest. ". . . the ark is taken . . . your sons are slain. . . ."

Eli fell backwards and died where he had so long slept—by the temple post.

8

Sparrow on the House Top

Ask any child for a thumbnail description of the Psalmist and what you get will likely go something like this: He killed Goliath. He was a shepherd. He could play a harp. In that order. The more mature image is probably pretty much the same, with some comment about Bathsheba thrown in.

The fact is that there are few more lonely and tumultuous lives recorded in the Bible. It's hard to realize that the writer of almost everybody's favorite Psalm, one which evokes images of gentle, munching sheep, placid streams and an almost visible surfeit of "goodness and mercy" following its sleek and well-fed beneficiaries, was likely an anguished fugitive when he penned its words.

In fact, David's chances for being a successful, socially well-adjusted human being were just about nil—from youth to old age. He was a lad who could have had a real identity problem. It wasn't just having to watch the sheep in the Judean hills surrounding his home town. Bethlehem itself was a nothing sort of place. Three hundred years later it would still be called by the Prophet Micah the least of all the Judean villages. What could ever happen in such a sleepy place to make a fellow's dreams come true or even to break a lively teenager's tedium?

Good looking, bright-eyed, husky, and possessed of a winsome personality, what dad wouldn't be proud of David? Someone had to watch those flocks, however, and if you were the youngest son among many older ones as he was, you must learn to take the leftovers in life. It was a healthy existence, wandering with the flocks in search of pasture and water by day and bedding down under the stars at night, wrapped in a sheepskin cloak. But it was a lonely life for a young, convivial fellow—totally without companionship except for his sheep and a simple peasant's lyre.

On a never-to-be-forgotten day, however, an excited servant came leaping over the rocks and hillocks to tell him he was wanted—immediately—at home. Breathlessly he explained that the Prophet Samuel had arrived that day at the city gates. How the elders of the town had trembled! Such visits usually marked either disasters or denunciations. He'd called instead for Jesse's sons and ordered them to attend him in a ceremonial sacrifice. Then he'd lined the boys up, the seven who were at home.

"David, would you believe it, he's come to anoint a new king! One of your *brothers*. *Your* brothers!" The honest face of the sweating servant lit up already with a new respect.

But the puzzlement was even greater than the pride. His father was waiting for him to be present, obviously so he could do his obeisance too. But was he really that important? Should he be allowed to leave the sheep? How exciting—and puzzling —it all was.

Nothing made sense when David arrived at the still-smoking altar and looked around. Samuel stood apart, solemn-faced and holding a vial of oil in one hand. The seven brothers looked chagrined—every one of them—and terribly displeased to see *him* there. And his father? He had a look of utter incredulity on his face.

Then it happened, so quickly that he was only aware of the fragrant oil running from his red hair and down his ruddy cheeks. "*You* are the one—the Lord's anointed. The throne of Israel is yours!"

It was a stunning announcement all around. Nothing in life had ever prepared David for *this*. He was so very expendable that he'd been overlooked in the most important conference ever to be called in that very ordinary family. When Samuel had commanded Jesse to summon all of his sons, that "all" hadn't even included him.

The event itself would have been easy to forget, too, since it was back to the flocks, on the double, when it was all over. The time hadn't yet come to assume power, and our young David went contentedly back to the hills. It must have seemed like a dream, but like Mary twenty-eight generations later, he kept these things in his heart.

All the while, just seven miles away, entirely unaware of the secret anointing or even of David's existence, Saul wore himself out in frustrated battle against the Philistines, even while he fought the increasing depression that drove him to the brink of madness. Someone suggested music to soothe his torments. What's more, they knew just the one to summon. He was sure to be available—merely a shepherd. So close by, too—just a few hills away. And so David was installed at Gibeah to drive away the evil spirits that tormented Israel's great king. Saul grew to love the unassuming lad and soon made him his armor-bearer as well. From shepherd to court musician and armor-bearer— it was quite a jump. But for a fellow who was the king-in-waiting it wasn't that much of an honor, especially when he still went back and forth to help out with the chores at home. Eventually, however, the soothing interludes had their desired effect. The musician was no longer needed and all was as it always had been.

The years that passed must have raised questions in young David's mind. Who was he—*really?* King or shepherd? Had it all been a dream? A mistake? His brothers would have him believe it. They'd all gone on to bigger and better things. Right now the three eldest were with their king, drawn up in battle array against the Philistines in the valley of Elah. It was another put-down for him when he went to visit them there with bread and cheese in hand and greetings from their father. We all know the story—David's outrage that none dared to accept the challenge of the heathen Goliath, and his brothers' displeasure that he'd leave the sheep to come with idle curiosity to view the battlefield. After all, this place was for valiant *men*, not boys. When mighty Goliath fell to the ground, with David's well-flung stone sunk in his forehead, Israel had an instant hero. Strange that Saul hadn't even recognized his beloved musician.

From that moment David was either loved or hated, lauded or hunted. Schooled in solitude, he would never again be a nonentity, even when he wanted nothing more than to be left alone in pious meditation on his God.

Eventually he did become a king, secure upon his throne, but only after years as a fugitive with a price on his head. From sheepfold to Adullam's cave to palace, it was a long and lonely road. At last with the kingdom won and secure from its enemies, the shepherd who loved the lyre and star-studded nights far better than the glories of war, had rest from his enemies. His longtime dream, to build a worthy house for God, however, was doomed to disappointment. "You're a man of war, David. Too much blood on your hands. Another will build it."

After that it was rebellion in his own household. "Oh, Absalom, my son, my son! If only I could have died for you!" he cried over the traitor when news of his death was brought. A final crisis over the succession hounded him to his deathbed, was solved, and David rested with his fathers at last, to bear forever the divine approval: "a man after God's own heart."

Just what did this man have to merit such a benediction? It's worth investigating. Let's go back to Psalm 23. What's the feeling you get? Peace, right? Just oceans of fathomless peace. It's a peace that flourishes in solitude. In fact, the only human beings around are the enemies in whose midst David sits at the well-prepared table. It's perhaps the most elusive commodity the world about us or the world within affords. It's so coveted that certain governments speak of waging peace. They pursue it with a vengeance and woo it with atrocious acts of war.

Individuals seek it to the ends of the earth—and out of it—in transcendental meditation, astral projection, or drug-induced euphoria.

Even a Christian doesn't get it automatically with salvation —that peace of God which passes understanding. The feel-good, everything-going-smoothly, ever-victorious brand of serenity is a deception and a fraud if it doesn't operate as well when things go awry. And if it worked for David, it can surely work for us, for never was a man more caught up in strife and turmoil, personal disappointment, false accusations, intrigues —you name it. At one time or another he felt all of the most devastating human emotions. If ever a man felt unloved, over-looked, alone, betrayed by friends, inadequate, misunderstood, or unappreciated, it was he. Do you ever think of him in this way? We all have our favorite Psalms, usually the praise or victory variety, but the fact is that most of them are a big cry for *help!* They weren't written during the leisure years of retire-ment and retrospect. They were wrenched out of his heart's core during the heat of battle, the despair of flight, or during moments of respite with new crises looming on the horizon. Listen:

> I am weary with my groaning . . . I water my couch with my tears. Mine eye is consumed because of grief; it waxeth old because of all mine enemies.
>
> Psalms 6:6,7

> Why standest thou afar off, O LORD? why hidest thou thyself in times of trouble?
>
> 10:1

> How long wilt thou forget me, O LORD? . . .
>
> 13:1

> Yea, mine own familiar friend, in whom I trusted, which did eat of my bread, hath lifted up his heel against me.
>
> 41:9

. . . refuge failed me; no man cared for my soul.

142:4

False witnesses did rise up; they laid to my charge things that I knew not.

35:11

For my life is spent with grief, and my years with sighing. . . . I was a reproach among all mine enemies, but especially among my neighbours. . . . I am forgotten as a dead man. . . .

31:10–12

He doesn't sound like either an invincible warrior or a man confidently sheltered in the arms of God, does he? And what comes through so clearly is that it wasn't the reverses in battle that bothered him so much. It was those seven deadly wounds that hurt: the feeling of being unloved, overlooked, alone, betrayed by friends, inadequate, misunderstood, and unappreciated. The sling and the bow he could handle, but it was the human injustices of life that destroyed his peace.

And so it is with us, too. It isn't the burned cake, the flat tire, or even the cost of living index that becomes intolerable. Those things make up good, acceptable kaffeeklatsch conversation, and by the telling lose some of their sting. There are those other things, the ones David experienced, that make a churning chaos of our inner lives. You fly into a rage because the sewing machine needle breaks, but what you're really mad about is that *he* never notices how hard you try to keep up your appearance —on a shoestring too. Junior gets an unmerited swat, because what really bugs you is that the Big Boss is somewhere on an expense account, and you're stuck in your own kitchen to eat a lonely dinner in company with his spitting image and the smell of cheap fish. Or how about having to smile through gritted teeth as everyone congratulates the grinning employee who's just landed the plum *you'd* counted on?

On and on we go, covering, maneuvering, wanting sympathy
—*not* wanting the exposure that the bestowing of that sympathy brings—suppressing the hurts and at the same time creating
new tensions as we try to camouflage the hurts. Of course we
can't say, "I feel so unappreciated . . . overlooked . . . lonely."
After all, to admit to being lonely would be to admit to a whole
set of contributing reasons for that social isolation—all of them
ugly: "I have no talents. I'm dull, boring, uneducated, a loser,
physically unattractive. Naturally no one cares for my company." And so the inner condemnation rests like a dead weight
on the spirit, even as the pain surfaces in the most bizarre
cover-ups.

How well I remember the tall, skinny girl that walked so
aloofly through the high-school dining-hall in the 1940s. It was
a long way from door to steam table, between the dozens of
tables of laughing, joking teenagers. She held her head high and
looked straight ahead, as if she couldn't care less about the
carefree laughter on either side. If ever a girl looked conceited,
it was this one. One day she caught the contemptuous words:
"Thinks she's so beautiful," from an aisle-side table—and almost dissolved in tears on the spot. I was that girl. It wasn't
feelings of conceit that were uppermost in my mind. It was the
daily fear that I wouldn't find a friend to sit by at the end of
that long walk that put the glazed and haughty look in my eye.
Who could have known?

At this point we can admire a candid spirit like David's.
Problems he had plenty of, but at least he didn't compound
them by a false facade of ever-victorious coping. "Nobody loves
me." Who'd ever say such a damning thing about themselves?
David would—and he did—with utter candor by admitting
exactly how he felt. And recorded it too.

What kind of lessons can we learn from this amazing man
who "tells all" with such disarming frankness? The basic one
is quite simply this—that for all the failure and fretting and
even fuming David knew where to turn in a crisis. He wasn't
an uncomfortable, bigger-than-life supersaint. Just a very hu-

man fellow with a very great God to turn to in his trouble. It explains the change from Psalm to Psalm.

> I'm like a pelican in the wilderness, an owl in the desert ... a sparrow alone on the house top. My enemies reproach me all the day ... I've eaten ashes like bread, and mixed my drink with weeping, Because of your indignation and anger: because you've lifted me up and knocked me down again. My days are like a shadow ... I'm withered like grass. *But* you, O LORD, shall endure forever ... you are the same, and your years have no end.
>
> *See* Psalms 102:6–12

Then the tempo quickens and David is off and running with a paean of praise to his God:

> Bless the LORD, O my soul: and all that is within me, bless his holy name. . . . Don't forget his benefits. Remember he's merciful and gracious. He won't always be angry. He's like a father who pities his children. He knows our limitations —that we're but dust.
>
> *See* Psalms 103:1–14

On and on he goes, shaking misery and loneliness as he burrows deep into the love of God. David had a Friend who would never fail nor forsake him, and of this he was dead sure.

How different David was from a recent generation of Christians who didn't dare admit to either failure or temptation. It would have been, Oh, so unspiritual and would have given the lie to the cult of ever-victorious Christian living. No matter that all the evidence pointed to something less than perfection in the life. One "took it by faith" and went one's way through fire and flood, weal or woe, with an ever-ready smile. How beautiful real serenity is, but never did David fake it for the sake of his self-image or to prove he had a special dispensation of grace from God. His recourse in sorrow and loneliness was solidly based on a *promise,* a *place* of communion, and an attitude of *praise.*

First the promise, without which nothing else could be valid. Years before the troubles came, at that first meeting between the aged Samuel and the young shepherd, the voice of God had come to the prophet with an authority that couldn't be denied. "Anoint him: for this is he." Instantly that obedience to the heavenly vision was sealed by the Holy Spirit and David was to carry forever after the assurance that his destiny as Israel's future king was fixed and God's promise immutable. That assurance had nothing to do with circumstances. Even Samuel could easily have been fooled. Eliab was a much more likely candidate for the job—an eldest son, tall, handsome, qualified in every way. David was a surprise all the way around.

What an antidote to loneliness that promise was. To be sure its fulfillment was a long time in coming. In the meanwhile, he went back to the sheep, to emerge briefly as court musician and armor-bearer to Saul. Then back to slay Goliath and a brief period of hero worship before Saul's implacable jealousy drove him out again. Then the loss of Jonathan, his one friend, and the life of a fugitive, first among the Philistines, then in company with his outlaw band in the forbidding wilderness of En-gedi on the edge of the Dead Sea. When twice David had Saul in his power and could have dispatched his tormentor, he proved that the promise of the kingdom included grace to wait until God's good time to claim it.

Are you waiting for the "crowning day" that's coming? Unappreciated, misunderstood, lonely, do you long for reassurance and security? Wait no longer. Those who have trusted Christ for salvation have been declared kings and priests unto God. It's a position that is as surely yours as if the crown rested already in its rightful place. Neither virtues nor graces nor outward appearance help or hinder. God uses the same measuring glance as He did with David and his apparently much better qualified brother Eliab—He looks on the heart. If that heart is committed to God you belong to the King. In fact, you *are* a king. That anointing of the Holy Spirit will carry you through both wilderness and warfare into the full possession of the kingdom.

For the Christian, the promises don't stop with the royal relationship. ". . . how shall he not with him also freely give us all things?" (Romans 8:32). And the certitude of these all things is just as great as with the initial gift. What Christian could live one moment in this mixed-up world without the certainty that all things do indeed work together for good if we're walking in the love of God? Corrie ten Boom relates the story of how she and her sister arrived at their Ravensbruck barracks to find the straw in the tiers of bunks infested with fleas. For two refined middle-aged Dutch spinsters it seemed intolerable, but Betsie insisted that they give thanks for *all* things—and that included fleas! Later they learned that it was these same despised fleas that had kept the guards consistently out of the barracks, enabling them to hold the Bible studies that brought comfort to so many of their fellow prisoners. That promise in Romans 8:28 is a royal promise for a royal child—already anointed and destined for the throne. Never forget it.

Life is tough. So full of temptations. David experienced it too. Remember Bathsheba? It's hard to resist the allurements of sin when it's flaunted so appealingly on every side. But listen: "He is able to keep you from falling, and to present you faultless before the presence of his glory with exceeding joy" (Jude v. 24). Do you believe it? Do you believe that the One who died to save you from eternal harm can keep you right now from Satan's power?

He was able but we weren't willing, and sin has come into our lives to destroy the joy and block our usefulness. That's covered with His beautiful promise too. "If we confess our sins, he is faithful and just to forgive us our sins, and to cleanse us from all unrighteousness" (1 John 1:9). We can go on chastened and renewed and restored to the joy of our salvation as David did.

Life has been one disappointment after another. Dreams remain unfulfilled. Friends forsake or betray—or even just pass on. Moth and rust corrupt and thieves break through and steal. You find you can't count on anyone or anything—anywhere. Comes the promise, ". . . I will *never* leave thee nor forsake thee" (Hebrews 13:5). Even when your faith is so weak you're not aware of My presence, I'll be there. "Whither shall I flee from thy presence (even if I wished to)," the Psalmist cried. "If I make my bed in hell, behold thou art there" (Psalms 139:8). He's been there—and understands—and cares. Does it matter?

Our lives are expendable. We're just one among so many. We're reminded daily and with increasing alarm that there are too many of us on this planet. Would anyone care if one day we just weren't around anymore? Sadly enough, for many the answer would be *no*. Somewhere there *has* to be something to cover the dread fear of dissolution. I'm all I have on this planet. Nothing much has happened that's right down here. I can't believe this is all there is—just a hope in this life. There's a promise to cover the final act too, before the curtain goes down. Listen:

> For we know that if our earthly house of this tabernacle were dissolved, we have a building of God, an house not made with hands, eternal in the heavens. . . . We are confident . . . and willing rather to be absent from the body, and to be present with the Lord."
>
> 2 Corinthians 5:1,8

O Death, where is your sting, with a promise like that?

One day the fighting and the fleeing were over and David did wear the promised crown. It didn't spell the end of trouble, and there were many times when David had to reassure himself of God's promise. Even his favorite son rebelled against him and died fighting against his father. There did come a time, however, when David had rest from his enemies. At last he could fulfill his dearest wish (or so he thought) to build a worthy house for God to which a grateful people could come for worship. It wasn't to be. David's hands were stained with too much blood. That task would have to wait for his son.

But—if David's dearest wish—to build God a house—was never realized, how explain the many references to a very special *place* where he apparently had frequent communion with God?

> "One thing have I desired of the LORD," he declared, "that will I seek after; that I may dwell in the *house* of the LORD all the days of my life, to behold the beauty of the LORD, and to enquire in his *temple*. For in the time of trouble he shall hide me in his *pavilion:* in the secret of his *tabernacle* shall he hide me. . . .
>
> Psalms 27:4,5

Definitely David was a very agile fellow to be in two places at once, since the Psalm was written in the heat of battle. "Though an host should encamp against me, my heart shall not fear: though war should rise against me, in this will I be confident" (27:3). Elsewhere David speaks of the beauties of this special "place" where he found sanctuary. How "amiable" this tabernacle is. How his heart longs for the courts of the Lord. Blessed are those who dwell there. (*See* Psalm 84.)

Quite simply, David had an ever-present place of retirement and renewal, even in the midst of battle, where he could meet with God. That place was just as available as God Himself. Home is where the heart is. His earthly home wasn't always tranquil. It was torn by domestic problems and in later years by rebellion. No wonder David felt like a sparrow on the house top. But he was a king with a promise to rely on and a place of sanctuary to rest in.

Without the *promise,* there could be no *place.* The trust that the first inspired opened the door to the latter. Shadrach, Meshach and Abed-nego were in this quiet place in the midst of the fiery furnace. Stephen was in this place of communion even as the stones struck him down. Paul was fellowshiping in joyous company with God in this same tabernacle while chained in a foul Roman prison.

"I go to prepare a place for you," Jesus promised as He took farewell of His disciples. That place would be real only in a future day. They had yet to learn the reality of the Comforter that He would send to them as a permanent resident in their hearts. The Holy Spirit who would fill that inner sanctuary would be a far more real and potent Presence for them than David ever knew. Do we complain of loneliness and not seek the place that David's heart longed for? The search must begin there.

It couldn't all be just rocklike reliance on a promise and the sweet place of prayer. All that security and serenity had to burst out somehow, and *praise* became the culminating element in David's experience. "It is a good thing to sing praises to our Lord," he says, and how right he is. To say *thank you* or to speak well of another is indeed a psychologically healthful exercise. It gets our minds off ourselves, for one thing, and if our lives are anything like David's we have need of this.

More than that, however, it's the only honest way to go. He is worthy. That's the theme of both angels and elders in the Book of Revelation, and will be throughout eternity. Surely we can find *one* thing—if not a hundred—to praise God for. David never ran out of praise material. For David no blessing was too small to give thanks for, nor anyone too insignificant to render it. Let *everything* that has breath praise Him.

Yes, praise is a command. The man who was so alone, misunderstood, unappreciated—and all the rest—actually sang himself into a fine state of getting it all together. It hardly seems possible that the wretch who felt like a sparrow alone on the

9

The God Who Is Not There

It was dark, appropriately so, the darkest night of Saul's life. Behind him his armies were pitched on Gilboa, ready to face the Philistines massed against them. With two servants, he crept stealthily along the scarcely discernible path that led to an isolated hut. This night Saul was disguised. Never must it be known that Israel's king, who by his own decree had outlawed the occult craft, was on his way to consult Endor's witch.

For Saul it was the ultimate loneliness. From the far side of an unbridgeable chasm he reached across to the God who was no longer there. He sought and he couldn't find. He knocked and no one answered. In an extremity of anguish he groped at the edge of the abyss, and like the shepherd lad who would sit on the throne after him, his cry must have been, "My God, my God, why hast Thou forsaken me?" David knew, however, that his cry of despair, uttered in a weak moment, was addressed to One who was there after all—One who would assuredly answer. ". . . be not silent to me:" David had pleaded, "lest . . . I become like them that go down into the pit." With him, it was a cry to a God who was definitely there and infinitely to be desired. He knew that no loss, whether it was the throne that had eluded him so long, or friends, or reputation, or life itself, could compare with the loss of that relationship. From the pit of hell there would be no answer, and it was just at the brink of that great fixed gulf that Saul trembled on this dark night.

That God's Spirit had once rested on Saul and had made His voice known made it all the more bitter. That guidance had assured success beyond his wildest dreams. Not only had God's Spirit come and gone according to the need, but there had been faithful Samuel to give him counsel and encouragement. Now Samuel was dead—the prophet who had anointed him to be king and deliverer of Israel, and whose counsel he'd once depended upon. The Philistines, whose destruction he'd been elevated to accomplish, were waiting for the kill right now. That thought haunted him. David, the sweet singer he'd once loved and knew would be king after him, was with those armies, anointed, and ready to take the vacant throne. That thought haunted him, too. The great things he'd been meant to accomplish for Israel tortured him. Everything had come full circle for him this night, and the worst of all was that there was nowhere to turn. No one to reach out a helping hand. No one even to confess to. In hell he lifted up his eyes and from an unfathomable distance saw everything that was really worthwhile and had once been his—or at least obtainable—totally and forever beyond reach. Only the powers of darkness were at his disposal now and he was helpless even to summon them without the aid of the despised woman to whom he was hurrying. Without God and without hope in this world, he merely went to have his doom confirmed. Hell.

What was a nice boy from Gibeah doing in a spot like this? What, after all, is anyone doing at the gates of hell? The ingredients of the tragedy are in most cases frighteningly similar: a very ordinary human being expected by man and society to perform in a capacity he was never designed for.

The emergency is and was real. Our present world is in a mess. Israel stood in grave peril then as it does now. The debacle of the ark's removal from Shiloh had had devastating results. Even after its recovery, the Philistines had continued their inroads, taking town after town in a series of demoralizing aggressions. With the death of Eli and his sons, Samuel had taken over the spiritual leadership of Israel, and in a dramatic display of divine power God had routed the Philistines at Mizpah. It was an affirmation of what God could do in answer to one man's righteous prayers. When the victories weren't immediately followed up, the demand came that sparked the disaster, ". . . appoint us a king to govern us like all the nations."

Poor Samuel. His first impulse was to feel sorry for himself. But no, God assured him, ". . . they have not rejected thee, but they have rejected me that I should not reign over them. . . . Yet protest solemnly unto them, and show them the manner of the king that shall reign over them."

That's where the isolation began with Eve. *Had God really said? (See* Genesis 3:1.) Wasn't there another way to go than total obedience? For the nation of Israel, Moses' deathbed charge and Joshua's challenge to decision at the entrance to the land, and now Samuel's warning, would add up to a monumental witness against the people, when those calamities of which each spoke would indeed fall on them. "And in that day you will cry out because of your king, whom you have chosen for yourselves; but the Lord will not answer you in that day."

Into this tragedy in the making fell Saul, and a more appropriately chosen victim you couldn't find. Good-looking, tall, a pleasing personality . . . he was all of these. Surely if the people must have a king, he was the best available. Still, he was no substitute for God and that's what the people wanted—and still do. Nevertheless, God was going to be with him. Samuel promised it . . . *if.* One of the big *ifs* had to do with obedience to God's prophet. "And the Spirit of the LORD will come upon thee, and thou shalt be turned into another man." Humbly Saul began by following directions. It was all so new.

It wouldn't be too difficult to replace Saul with any of today's millions of bewildered "kings" who are trying to rule a personal universe that they were never meant to have dominion over.

With all the looks, talent, and good intentions in the world, Saul knew he didn't have enough to make it, and on the day of his presentation to the tribes he hid. It was quite possibly the most totally honest act of his life.

Sin was no new thing in Israel's national life. It isn't an isolated occurrence in ours either. But Israel's king was already a fact when Samuel's final grim forecast was made. (*See* I Samuel 12:13–15.) Though the people were smitten with remorse, it was too late to remedy the evil. Still, there was an out. "Fear not: ye have done all this wickedness: yet turn not aside from following the LORD." Graciously Samuel continued to comfort his conscience-stricken people. ". . . God forbid that I should sin against the LORD in ceasing to pray for you . . . Only fear the LORD, and serve him in truth with all your heart: for consider how great things he hath done for you. But if ye shall still do wickedly, ye shall be consumed, both ye and your king."

It wasn't too auspicious a beginning for the young seeker of asses from Gibeah, but nevertheless God's promise of help rested upon him if he'd pick up the already marred fabric of the new kingdom and walk in humble dependence upon God.

How often we, too, have to pick up the broken pieces that even a confessed sin leaves. God *does* help us to cope with the wreckage, and with His beautiful *if* He presents a way of escape. As Samuel prayed for Israel, there is One who prays for us with groanings which cannot be uttered. And then there is God's promise as it came on this occasion: "For the Lord will not forsake his people for his great name's sake: because it hath pleased the Lord to make you his people" (1 Samuel 12:22). The reliability and glory of God's own name is at stake in the quality of help He gives. Add to that the pleasure He gets in making us His. He won't be robbed of that divine pride of ownership. *Nothing* shall separate us from the love of God—ever. Neither would the Son allow anything to come between Himself and the joy that was set before Him in having us forever in His keeping.

With all the certainty of God's love to bolster and all the skill of the Great Physician to heal, we too can turn even a tragic mistake into a point of departure for a deeper and more chastened walk with Him.

Granted Saul was in an uncomfortable spot—in fact, in the spot that only God should occupy. Still, He was faithful to His promise, and the electorate's choice began his reign with all the popularity and goodwill that a new king could well expect. Could we stretch the point enough to suggest that he occupied just about the same position as a new Christian born into a marred world? It isn't the best of all possible worlds. That one was left behind long ago in the Garden. But it's the one we *have,* and with the help of the Holy Spirit to guide and Jesus to stand surety to God's promises, we actually can make it. Saul definitely wasn't alone in this problem-riddled situation.

How important the first steps are for an infant. Compulsively it clutches the outstretched hand. How terrifying the small, small world is from the height of those two chubby and now-upright legs. The infant dares because Mother is there, or Dad. We dare walk in this marred universe only because the Holy Spirit provides that helping ministry for us the moment we're born into God's family. We're not left alone. Any separation thereafter is by our own choosing. Saul's link with God and everything right in Israel's national life depended upon obedience—the *if* that spelled the difference between disaster and success.

It didn't take long for the man who had everything, except the right to rule, to alienate himself from the help he needed. A crucial battle with the Philistines loomed. The instructions were clear. Saul was to draw up his armies, to present an offering and enquire of the Lord. The days passed. When Samuel didn't appear, Saul's men panicked and scattered. Saul couldn't wait. Militarily the time for attack was right, and to get on with the action Saul offered the sacrifice himself. When Samuel did appear, the excuses fell flat. Foolish Saul. The rule was his only *under* God. He is no fool who gives up what he cannot keep, whether it involves the ordering of one's own affairs or those of a kingdom. Both realms were lost to Saul that day. Thereafter it was ". . . war against the Philistines all the days of Saul."

Is this the story of your life? War—nothing but total and unremitting warfare? Life *is* a battle. We're told that. But we were never meant to fight the good fight of faith alone. Equipped with a will, we can say *yes* or *no* or *maybe* or *someday*. Saul took a calculated risk that day. "My good sense against Yours, Lord. My armies are scattering. Samuel is lingering. I'll take his place this once and do what *I* think is *best!*" Oh, yes, Saul thought it was best. It made all the sense in the world—that act of disobedience. Poor, miscast Saul—and Joe, and Sam, and Jane.

It had been a mini-test with dynamic repercussions. Part of Saul's hell was knowing exactly what to expect. When shorn Samson awoke on the knees of Delilah with the Philistines surrounding him, he didn't know his strength had departed. When Saul took the field next, he knew he'd lost the battle already, if not the war.

The final rupture in Saul's lifeline to guidance came when he failed to utterly destroy the Amalekites. Their armies he beat —all the pesky little fellows that scurried across the battlefield and weren't any match for Saul's well-drilled armies anyway. It was the king he spared, though, the one who had the power to direct and command and influence. He and the best of his goods he spared. Nothing vile or shoddy or reprehensible for Saul. No, just the sins of quality—the kind that only Lucifer, the Son of the Morning, would think of tempting him with.

That night saw Agag, king of the Amalekites, dead by Samuel's hand, and the angry prophet gone up to Ramah to stay. In Saul's hand lay his torn mantle, a visible reminder of Samuel's prophecy: the kingdom was already as good as in the hands of David. Better to be hunting asses still.

THE GOD WHO IS NOT THERE

It's been said that one of the more exquisite tortures of hell is the realization of what might have been. From the time that the evil spirit from God began troubling Saul, there were dangled before his vision, in the shape of David, all the beautiful impossibilities. The lad with the sling, or the harp, or the song outclassed him every time. Fear gripped Saul's heart because he saw that the God who had forsaken him was now with David. It was no contest.

From now on it was the vain and often ludicrous pursuit of what had already been lost. The close fellowship of one who is walking in God's favor isn't too welcome a sight for any of us when we're out of touch ourselves. And if that person is kind to us in our need it's doubly painful. Saul found David's magnanimity when he had Saul in his power unendurable.

"My lord the king," David respectfully addressed him. *But for how long?* "I will not put forth my hand against the Lord's anointed," David declared. *That's generous, but I'm not the Lord's anointed anymore.*

The gracious words seared Saul's conscience. He had known the quality of God's mercy. It was being reproduced in the one who would take his place upon the throne. Understandably it was hard to say *please* and *thank you*.

"After whom doest thou pursue? After a flea?" David appealed. *Yes, and you're just as elusive. I'll never catch you, and still I'll pursue.*

Saul wept. What else was there to do? One last request. It was that his house might not be destroyed, though he should die. It was the plea of defeat. With David's solemn promise the broken king turned homeward.

Once again these two met—in similar circumstance. Unbelievable that Saul, the morally vanquished king, should bless the one he pursued and reaffirm his right to reign. He seemed to be marking time at the gates of hell.

Literature is full of the less-than-tranquil statements of men who stand alone at the hour of death. Addressing the one he didn't believe in, Voltaire cried, "O Christ! O Lord Jesus! I must die—abandoned of God and of men!" "Send even a child to stay with me, for it is hell to be alone!" Thomas Paine cried out in his death agony. For the atheist Thomas Hobbes, death was "a great leap in the dark." The darkness of first Creation was bleak enough, but then there was no living soul to feel it. God dispelled that darkness and prepared the earth before He ever placed man here. That darkness descends again when man cuts himself off from the light.

In the darkness of the witch's hut, Saul knew the alienation from one's Creator that cancels everything else out. What does it profit a man if he gains the whole world and loses his own soul? The news Saul learned that night denied him even a small part of that world. All the mighty exploits and even the time taken from the battle to track the fugitive David wouldn't make the slightest difference when he and his sons lay dead on the battlefield the next day. It was Samuel's last message. The prophet whom the witch had called up from the dead couldn't resist a final dig. "What's the point of asking me for advice if God Himself won't speak to you?"

It took all the persuasive powers of the despised but compassionate witch to get Saul on his feet again. However terrible it was to know the magnanimity of David, it must have been more than humiliating for the King of Israel to sit on a bed in a smoky mountain hut, being persuaded to down a hastily prepared meal by the solicitous woman who knew his terrible secret.

The final battle was a matter of going through the motions —a ritual which finalized what had been decreed long ago. In this context it's easy to see how those outside Christ are dead in trespasses and sins. He that doesn't believe is "condemned already"—a life in death. Eternity without Christ *has* begun for those who refuse Him. There could scarcely be a more pitiful figure in all the world than the disguised Saul staggering back into the night to face a battle that was already lost. He'd have to put on a good front tomorrow. Review the troops. Harangue his men. Inspire them with courage. Lead the charge. And die.

Is this *all* there is to life, and is this really the way to die? The Bible speaks of another death—the death to self that awakens life. It means the rooting out of Amalek, the sin principle. The Bible speaks of One whose right it is to reign and who is equipped for the job. It speaks, too, of a choice to be made and of the consequences when man tries to manage that kingdom on his own. It was voiced by Moses as a death charge, before the children of Israel crossed the Jordan, that symbol for us of our entrance into our own Christian heritage.

> See, I have set before thee this day life and good, and death and evil; In that I command thee this day to love the LORD thy God, to walk in his ways, and to keep his commandments and his statutes and his judgments, that thou mayest live . . . But if [thou] turn away, so that thou wilt not hear . . . I denounce unto you this day, that ye shall surely perish . . . I call heaven and earth to record this day against you, that I have set before you life and death, blessing and cursing: *therefore choose life.* . . .
>
> Deuteronomy 30:15–19

Saul suffered the only kind of loneliness that God in His Word guarantees we need never feel. No lack of self-esteem for him, or prestige or admiring friends. Just the alienation, by choice, of the One whose presence makes every other loss endurable, even of life itself.

10

"You Let Me Down, Lord!"

With purposeful step the solitary figure strode from the colossal hilltop palace. He had no eyes for the magnificent "house of ivory" he was leaving, so named because of its fabulous decor imported from nearby Tyre. From that same Phoenician trading center had come its painted and Baal-worshiping mistress, Ahab's queen, the infamous Jezebel. The loincloth-clad figure with the stern, unbending gaze had just come from the king's audience chamber—and what an audience it had been!

"As the Lord God of Israel liveth, before whom I stand, there shall not be dew nor rain these years, but according to my word!"

The king hadn't answered a word to the thunderous pronouncement. Exactly the way it should be. Since the division of the kingdom after Solomon's death, there hadn't been one decent king on Israel's throne, and now this Ahab—he was surely the worst, though it was his heathen queen, with her personal retinue of 450 prophets brought with her from Tyre that had really prompted today's visit. Not only were these parasites fed and housed at public expense in the royal palace, but Ahab had built a temple nearby in this capital city of Samaria, where they performed the vile rites which supposedly made prosperous and fertile the land. But this day Elijah had laid it on the line. Not Baal, but Jehovah God, controlled the clouds and wind and rain. Elijah was out to prove it. Ahab's face had blanched, then flushed with anger. But he hadn't said a word. Likely he'd run to Jezebel as soon as he recovered his wits.

Now *there* was a woman to reckon with. The sophisticated, worldly queen looked down on the simpler, more primitive Israelites. She took no pains to endear herself to the people; took none to ingratiate herself with her husband either, Elijah suspected. Ahab was bad enough on his own, but with this woman behind him he was a monster.

With a smug look of satisfaction Elijah swept deliberately through the marketplace, out the huge covered gateway that pierced the thick city walls, then past the small, rough-hewn stone houses that clung so closely to the outer citadel wall. After an announcement like that, another man would have been on the run, but not this fearless prophet.

Elijah was headed for a three-year parenthesis that was really just an extension of what life had always been like for him. His friends—or should we say his acquaintances—even suspected that he rather liked it that way. Prophets were never loved. Feared, yes. Perhaps even admired. But those who had to tell it like it was were never very popular in those days, when "like it was" always meant bad news. The medicine he had to dispense always seemed to be given with a certain relish. Ironic that he should hail from the province of Gilead, famous for the soothing and aromatic resins extracted from its fragrant herbs. The medicine he brought from Gilead, however, was right now sure to be causing an angry uproar in the royal palace that was receding into the distance behind him.

"What a man!" we say. Being a disliked loner takes a bit of guts even for a Christian. To be the forerunner of a long line of angry prophets just wouldn't be everybody's cup of tea. God knew His man, however, and we confront in Elijah one of those rare individuals who seem to fit the role as easily as his gnarled feet fit the sturdy sandals that were even now carrying him toward the hideout God had prepared for him on an isolated tributary of the Jordan River.

Few of us could imagine ourselves wearing Elijah's mantle. The image isn't flattering, for one thing, and we can't quite place ourselves in such a grim context. Of course, we concede, there *must* be the lonely voices in the wilderness, the unwelcome Cassandras who never seem acquainted with anything positive or pleasant to pass along, the prophets of doom who see only the dark side of every silver lining. "But that just doesn't fit my personality, Lord—You know I have different gifts." With that helpful reminder off our chests, we back away from that God-given sense of outrage that sees sin as God sees it.

All of us must be lonely in this way sometimes. There are times when there's no one else to help or support and, like Daniel, we must dare to stand alone for an unpopular cause. The commitment to ugly truth can spell the end to a promising political career, or it can make Dad a very unpopular person right in his own home, at least until the peaceable fruits of righteousness, which are the end product of the confrontation, take over.

It doesn't take too much adjustment of the indignant prophet's declaration to put it right into the twentieth-century American family room. "As the Lord God of Israel lives, before whom I stand, you shall not have the family car, but according to my conditions." Sacrilege? Not at all. Are we sure, before God, that those conditions are just and fair? Then have an Elijah's courage and pronounce them. The result may be openmouthed wonder, but the chances are that you, like Elijah, will come out of it all with dignity, though you may have to sit by your own Cherith and wait for the Lord's final out-working of the problem. It took a very close walk with God to make Elijah so dead sure of what he was saying. When "my word" is *His* Word, I'm speaking with an authority so invincible that it hardly matters *who* I'm talking to (Ahab), what I'm wearing (a peasant's loincloth), or what happens next (like a three-year detour into the desert).

From adrenalin-charged action to sitting day after day and week after week by a slowly drying-up creek must have been a trial to the man designed for action. No languid Eli content to hold up the temple post, Elijah faced perhaps a bigger test in the wilderness than he did in Ahab's ivory palace. Gone was the stimulation of abrasive contact and the awesome sense of having power with God and men. Now it was sitting time. Who could devise a more clever form of torture for a fellow like Elijah? But here, too, he passed the test. No panic at the strange way of getting his groceries. No desperate outcry when the brook started drying up. Just a supreme confidence that this dismal place was exactly what the Lord had in mind for him at the moment.

Did Elijah use his time creatively? We don't know. Time to think he certainly had plenty of. Did he know God's magnificent promise to Jacob? "And, behold I am with thee, and will keep thee in all places whither thou goest, and will bring thee again into this land; for I will not leave thee, until I have done that which I have spoken to thee of" (Genesis 28:15). One would almost think so. That was food for thought to go with the ravens' daily gift.

The creativity of solitude is a theme that recurs again and again in the Bible. Moses spoke to God face-to-face in the mountain. John heard things unlawful for a man to utter on Patmos. Paul didn't confer with flesh and blood nor go up to Jerusalem to the apostles, but went into the solitary places of Arabia, where the Son was revealed in him. Handel's *Messiah* was conceived in solitude (as was Hitler's *Mein Kampf*). Jesus Himself withdrew from human companionship in order to commune with His Father and renew His spiritual dynamics. The lonely places are not ciphers in our lives when they cause us to wait upon God.

There came a time, however, when Elijah again became a man of action. Before his eyes the brook dwindled, until one day God announced his new assignment. Off to Zarephath and the home of an indigent widow and her young son. Again Elijah could exercise the role he loved best.

"Fetch me a drink." She fetched.

"Bring me some bread." The demand followed on the heels of the first even as she hurried to bring a drink. But this time there was no bread to bring. Only a bit of flour and a few drops of oil remained of her famine-ravaged supplies. It was enough for a last meal for her young son.

"Make me a cake first. Never fear. You'll lack for nothing from this day until the rains come again." She baked.

What superb confidence. What a sense of God's presence. The second test was passed with flying colors. But then, was it really that hard for a man who seemed to be made for this sort of thing?

Nothing chummy about the threesome. No comfortable little evenings spent in genial pleasantries. He was "a man of God," she a poor "widow woman"—and never would the twain meet except as master and servant. Her tearful accusation when her young son sickened and died delineated the gulf. . . . "What have I to do with thee, O thou man of God . . . art thou come to slay my son?"

Elijah's only answer was another order: "Give me thy son." When he was returned, restored to life, Elijah's third test was complete, his reputation as a "man of God" intact and enhanced. Awe and respect there must have been—but *love?* We get the feeling that he wasn't a man to inspire that sort of thing nor perhaps even to miss it.

But the grandeur of the lonely years was just a prelude to life's ultimate moment—a mountaintop experience to rival that of Moses. Back at the palace Elijah's bitter medicine was more unpalatable than ever. Between searching for Elijah and looking for water, Ahab had been a busy and an angry man indeed.

But when the time for a confrontation came, it was Elijah who summoned Ahab. And he came just as obediently as the widow had jumped to bring him his breakfast. Ahab's one brave attempt to intimidate this man was totally squelched. "No, *I'm* not the one who's troubling the land. *You* are! Now go and gather all of Israel and your prophets together on Mount Carmel." No explanation. Just *"Go!"*

Ahab went.

On the day appointed, thousands of hungry, thirsty, curious, more-than-a-little apprehensive Israelites pressed up the hills leading to the high mountains towering over the parched plains of the Jezreel Valley. They craned their necks to get a view of the drama unfolding on Carmel's summit. In one cluster were the 450 prophets of Jezebel, already in disrepute for their impotence in the face of three years of drought. Standing alone, but with all the aplomb of a five-star general with a division at his back, stood Elijah.

"How long will you go limping between two opinions? If the Lord is God, follow Him: but if Baal, then follow him."

In the profound silence that followed he laid out the conditions. "I'm the only one on God's side. You have 450 prophets standing there." (The handicap seemed generous enough.) "They'll prepare an altar and a sacrifice. I'll do the same. The God who answers by fire, let him be God."

Fair enough. The people responded enthusiastically. Ahab hadn't a word to say. The prophets could hardly complain.

That afternoon made all of Elijah's previous life worth living. With supreme confidence he looked on as the priests of Baal appealed to their god with increasing frenzy. Their reputation, their jobs, their very lives had been put on the block by this goatskin-clad nobody with the gargantuan-size gall. How had he pushed them into a showdown like this anyway? How had Ahab dared to allow it? Jezebel believed in them, but she was back at Jezreel's summer palace waiting for news.

As the day wore on, it became increasingly obvious that it

wasn't going to be a good scene. Not for them. In a frenzy, they slashed their bodies with knives. The people out there, pressing in so close, looked skeptical, angry—then downright danger-ous.

"Scream louder. Perhaps Baal is sleeping . . . or on a jour-ney."

The derisive voice of Elijah, as he stood so serenely still, was taken up and mimicked from mouth to mouth. In despair the haggard priests threw down their swords and knives in defeat and huddled together beside the unconsumed pyre.

It was Elijah's turn. With deliberate care he erected an altar of twelve stones, dug a trench about it, laid the wood in order and placed the slain bullock on top. Was it now ready? No. In wide-eyed wonder the crowd pressed in to watch barrel after barrel of precious water being poured over the altar, until it filled the surrounding trench.

It was late in the afternoon when Elijah at last drew near to the altar and addressed himself in simple terms to the God who had for so long been his intimate and sometimes his only com-panion.

"Lord, let these people know that You're the God of Israel and that You're the one who has commanded these things. Hear me, O Lord, hear me."

In a matter of moments the answering holocaust of fire had obliterated stones, bullock, wood, the very water around the altar. In terror the people fell back, crying, "The Lord, He is the God; the Lord, He is the God!"

We pause with Elijah at this moment of total triumph. Black-ened earth, nothing more, where pyre had once stood before him, faces transfixed in awe around him, cowering priests be-hind—the whole scene hung suspended in time and space upon Carmel's sunset-washed summit. Off to one side, alone, Ahab darted uncertain glances right and left. He hardly counted in that whole panorama and knew it. At that moment he feared Elijah even more than he hated him.

"Seize the prophets!" Elijah's order galvanized the crowd to action. Every last one was dragged down to the brook Kishon. Soon it ran blood-red to the valley below.

Elijah had proved his power—with God and with men. The months in lonely waiting beside the drying brook, those spent in the mean and parsimonious household of Zarephath's widow, were all forgotten. Mount Carmel was like a benediction on all his hard and abrasive life. One more thing remained to wrap it all up and this was sure to be crowned with success too.

"Eat, drink, Ahab. It's going to rain." The announcement allowed no doubt.

An order now to his servant. "Go back up the mountain. Tell me what you see."

Seven times his servant went and came before he had the news Elijah was waiting for.

"A small cloud—just a tiny one, master."

This was it. "Hurry, Ahab! Get off this mountain! *It's going to pour!*"

Gone the dignity, the self-contained majesty, the awesome solemnity. While Ahab climbed obediently into his chariot, Elijah prepared for the run of his life. It was the only way to express the triumph of this hour. Even before the last bloody folds of his mantle had been tucked into his girdle, he was off and running. Wildly, jubilantly, with giant leaps and bounds he cleared the rocks and brush in his path. On to Jezreel. Straight to the king's summer palace to confront the painted queen who'd seduced God's people. Oh . . . when she heard what had happened to her precious prophets! When she saw the darkening sky . . . felt the pelting drops! Elijah could see it all.

The beautiful vision lent wings to his feet as he flew down the mountain, across the plain and through the city gates. She'd cry out for mercy . . . confess before all Israel. Ahab, too. He, Elijah, would announce to the people the total triumph of Jehovah's cause. There would be a national revival. Israel's enemies would be paralyzed. The whole world would be turned upside down. Oh, glory, glory! What a testimony he'd have around the altars that would arise newly built throughout Israel. Elijah felt bigger than life when he strode through the giant doors of the palace to await the summons that would bring him into *her* presence.

Sometime later the curious who gathered at the palace steps looked in awestruck dismay as a rough-clad figure slunk out the great paneled doors and hurried away. *"Elijah?"* It couldn't be! But it was. How small he looked. He was as white as a sheet. Those closest passed the word.

"She's out to get him . . . swears revenge for her priests. He better move—fast."

Away Elijah hurried, incredulous—stunned. The ignominy of it all. Bested by this heathen woman. Everything had gone without a hitch until—*this*. The man who had short hours before ordered the whole contingent of prophets and priests slain, slunk through the gathering gloom. He was scared to death. And terribly disappointed in God.

One hundred and thirty miles into the wilderness Elijah fled to fling himself down at last under the sparse shade of a juniper bush. "O Lord, take away my life! I'm no better than my fathers."

Finished, Elijah's whole world had wound down to a grinding halt. He was nothing . . . no better than any of the long line of nobodies that made up his family tree. Carmel's smashing success had been just a tease after all, to leave him stranded at his most crucial hour. In total defeat Elijah curled up and went to sleep.

From Carmel's height to juniper bush—how many of us have taken that lonely road? We've also called the fire down. Perhaps it's a beautiful and well-ordered family, responsive, spiritually oriented, obviously a tribute in men's eyes to wise and loving training. But then along comes Junior, a maverick from the word *no*. With him the fire just doesn't ignite. Rebellious, stubborn, he's an embarrassment and a blot on the family reputation. Lord, how could You? Or it's the productive life that's been an inspiration to so many. The tireless campaigns that have yielded scores of converts, the books written, the seminars conducted, the interviews granted, the encounters with the great and near-great that have enhanced the cause of Christ. Then the whisper of unfounded scandal that looses the poison of bad publicity and a loss of momentum. "You've let me down, Lord—such a foolish, *preventable* thing, too."

Like Elijah, we've performed well, even nobly. Our lives have been geared to spiritual warfare and we've fought a good fight —and often alone. In fact, it's been rather stimulating to be the only one on the front lines. Unlike modest and apprehensive Jeremiah or Moses, we really *enjoy* the hue and cry of battle. The commands given in the name of the Lord have the ring of authority and, as with the widow of Zarephath, the response follows instantly on the heels of the order.

And then—Jezebel. The time when *it didn't work.* Of course for Elijah it was pretty awful to be intimidated by a woman. That was tough for his kind, nothing short of shattering, especially when he thought he'd annihilate her rebellious spirit just as he'd slain her prophets. But first and foremost, as he lay under the juniper tree, was the bitter thought that he'd been robbed—definitely—by a God who could have done so much better by him. Twice the well-rehearsed speech was ventured. "I've been jealous for You, Lord—the only one, too—and You let me down back there at the palace. Your one and only faithful servant."

Nobody was listening.

Elijah had always judged God's presence by the spectacular —and by its predictability. We can imagine Elijah on Carmel, nearly obliterated by smoke and soot. "Praise God! *It worked!* I've done it again! He is the Victor . . . Deliverer . . . the Lord He is the God—just like the people said." How easily the praise comes. But what is His name when I'm discouraged, defeated,

bucking life's contrary circumstances alone? Do I pat Him on
the back and dispense praise only when I'm pleased that He's
performed according to my will? He *never* changes. Isn't He
victor at *all* times?

God had to teach Elijah, not by fire, wind, or earthquake, but
in a whisper, that one so-called success does not insure another,
nor does it even enhance the name of the One who is all-wise
and holy from eternity. In our own lives it can become an
insidious form of dictating to God, especially if, like Elijah,
giving orders comes naturally. The pride of being essential was,
after all, just a step away from Lucifer's grasping sin. "You
need me, Lord. In fact, I'm all You've got!" God calls to us in
our self-pity and in our distorted self-view just as He did to
Elijah. "What are you doing here? Is it a total wipe-out because
I haven't performed just as you thought I should?"

The road to healing for Elijah was first of all food. How
beautifully practical. He'd been hit in his vulnerable spot and
God knew just how much he could take without a miraculously
supplied feast. Then it was on to Horeb, Moses' own mountain,
for the first real confrontation with God of his life.

Another surprise. God hadn't disqualified him from future
service because of his failure. And of course, by now, Elijah was
beginning to see that God hadn't let him down back there at
Jezreel either. As God had revealed Himself to Moses in a
burning bush—fiercely burning yet not consumed—so He was
revealing Himself to Elijah in a searing experience that did *not*
spell the end of his usefulness.

Up, Elijah! On to Damascus. Anoint kings over Syria and
Israel. Appoint Elisha as your successor. Get ready to meet
Ahab in a mighty victory. On your feet! You'll outlive your
enemy yet.

Elijah did come out of it all in one piece. In fact, he gained
a beautiful dimension of living he'd never had before. Not one
whit less courageous (remember, Naboth's vineyard was yet to
come), Elijah discovered that there was something far better

—and Darius'—and Cyrus', he has to be the strangest figure ever to appear in public life. When he was taken along with a large contingent of Jewish youths, the conquering king ordered the choicest of these young captives to accompany the sacred temple vessels to his far-off kingdom. It was loot fit to grace both the victor's palace and the treasure-house of his god, for these young men had been handpicked to enjoy some very special privileges in exchange for being decorative and intelligent. By express order of the king, they were to dine on food from the king's own table. Before three years were up, his captives would be both sleekly filled out and well indoctrinated in the ways of Babylon. How charitable Nebuchadnezzar must have thought he was. How prudent and wise. Perhaps there'd even be something to be learned from *their* barbaric culture. Surely these superb specimens must be aware that they were the luckiest captives ever to come out of a Babylonian raid alive.

When the choicest one of all, Daniel, the one the prince of eunuchs had renamed Belteshazzar, went on a hunger strike and refused both food and drink, there was a small uproar behind the scenes. All of the other Hebrew captives were happy to share the delicious bounty of the king's table—so why should this one complain that some of it had been offered to idols and included things Israel's God had labeled *unclean?* This was *Babylon*—not Jerusalem.

"You want me to get into trouble? After all I've done for you?" It was the prince pleading with his favorite. "Besides, you don't *do* this to the king—Nebuchadnezzar, yet. Be a good fellow and eat."

Young Daniel shook his head firmly and with that shake of the head he established his place in history as the man who dared to stand *alone.* No amount of persuasion could make him accept any compromising favors from Nebuchadnezzar.

But he *was* a good fellow, as the prince had said, and when his personal guard, the good-natured Melzar, appeared, Daniel won him over with a simple proposal. "Nothing but gruel for ten days. Then take a look. See if I and my friends don't survive as well on that. Just try us."

Of course we know the result. The four lads couldn't have looked fresher or more fit at the end of the trial. Nor did a steady diet of the tasteless grain diminish their qualifications to stand before the king. When three years were up, it was Nebuchadnezzar who was captivated. They'd be useful, these four, especially young Daniel. It was far more than native intelligence he possessed. There was a hidden source of power there that could put the king's own royal magicians and astrologers out of a job. Yes, Daniel was going to be very useful—*and* a bargain to feed, too.

We, too, are in Babylon, unwillingly in a world which sometimes treats its favorites very well indeed—for a price. The adjustment to its value system is undeniably tempting. Babylon was a far more sophisticated environment than any to be found in simple Judea. The king's meat had all the allurements of the forbidden fruit of Eden. And when one adds to the aroma and the visual impact of something we want very much the fact that we're terribly hungry, the stage is set for a king-size downfall. Jesus Himself was tempted just at that vulnerable juncture, too.

The fact is that with all the incentives pointed in the direction of compromise, Daniel depended on a decision. Once taken, he locked it in his heart, never to take it out for reexamination. No doubt there were times of temptation. Everybody was doing it. Who, after all, would know or care back home? A person had to live. What was really so wrong with a good meal anyway? The beautiful alternative floated before his vision—and nostrils. But there'd been a decision. He'd rest on that until the time of temptation was past. It was the kind of habit, or automatic reflex, that *wasn't* a sign of weakness. It was the emergency brake kept in reserve for the time when the rest of the mechanism wasn't functioning.

Are we aliens in our world? Noticeably? More likely we're pursuing a comfortable and well-adjusted life-style rather than acting like strangers and pilgrims who have here no continuing city. Far from adjusting, we're commanded to keep ourselves unspotted from the world. The question for us is whether as Christians we can be happy in the world without the world's "good things" of life. Torrey took a look around in his day and came to the conclusion that most Christians have just enough religion to make them miserable. They can't be happy giving themselves completely to the world because it bothers the conscience; nor can they be happy giving themselves completely to Christ, for fear they'll miss out on the fun.

Without a definite decision the agony will never be resolved. Am I missing something worthwhile? Who, after all, would care? Once won't hurt. Everybody else. . . . The rationalizations leap to our assistance. But what a difference a decision makes. A well-known twentieth-century martyr in an East European country determined to preach as God directed him in defiance of orders. He got what he expected when he was arrested—a stunning prison term of eight years in solitary. And what did he do when the joy of the Lord couldn't be contained during those lonely years? He danced. A ludicrous figure, emaciated, sick, in flapping prison garb—he danced.

Madam Guyon reflected a quieter exuberance when she wrote from a seventeenth-century cell:

> A little bird I am,
>   Shut from the fields of air;
> And in my cage I sit and sing
>   To Him Who placed me there;
> Well pleased a prisoner to be,
> Because, my God, it pleases Thee.
>
> My cage confines me round;
>   Abroad I cannot fly;
> But though my wing is closely bound,
>   My heart's at liberty;

My prison walls cannot control
The flight, the freedom of the soul.

Oh, it is good to soar
    These bolts and bars above,
To Him Whose purpose I adore,
    Whose providence I love;
And in Thy mighty will to find
The joy, the freedom of the mind.

Richard Wurmbrand didn't have many options in his prison cell—but he could express his heart's adoration for Christ. Madame Guyon was certainly limited in her choices, but she could sing praises to her faithful God. Daniel was a captive, too, but no one could come between him and his determination to keep himself pure and undefiled. A captive, he refused to act like one.

Perhaps the rare brand of separation that Daniel achieved is a lot more available than most of us dream. "If any man *will* come after me, let him deny himself, and take up his cross, and follow me," Christ said in Matthew 16:24. There's liberty! Do you *want* to follow Christ in obedient discipleship? Then do it. "Any man" means *you* just as much as the whosoever that may receive salvation through believing. Following Christ must begin with an act of the will. The whole might of the Babylonian Empire couldn't move Daniel when he faced his decision. Neither can anything in the world—nor out of it—stand in our way when we truly want to live a life untouched by the corruption of this world.

Significant is the fact that Daniel took the initiative, even though he was in enemy territory, and even though it meant the loneliness of standing for God against the crowd. With a hundred other captives he could have been happily feasting on delicacies he'd never dreamed of at home. None to criticize, all congratulating themselves on what a soft berth they'd found for themselves in Babylon. What a delightful surprise that life in this strange land could be so congenial after all. No doubt before long they wouldn't even be recognized on the streets as aliens.

Do we recognize the picture? Men *knew* that the disciples had been with Jesus. That contact had altered every look, word, and deed. Without opening their mouths they preached. Without lifting a finger they compelled men. Like them, we too are witnesses to the uttermost parts of the earth. From head to toe, whatever we're doing, good or bad or indifferent; whatever we're saying, we *are* sending signals that are being read and interpreted by a watching world.

Every one of the handpicked young men of Nebuchadnezzar's court was a witness. Those who took the initiative survived to make an impact for God that has lasted to our day. Those who had chosen to accommodate themselves to the exigencies of the moment faded from view. Useless, forgotten, without testimony, they totally lost their identity as witnesses for Israel's God.

How about the issue? Food. It seemed so paltry. Was it worth risking Daniel's head for? Another question then. How *was* he to be a standout in the crowd—and stand out he must if he were to preserve a testimony for God. Ethnically he wasn't too different. He couldn't distinguish himself by making his yearly pilgrimage to Jerusalem. He was too big an investment to stand in peril of his life. Determined to make a point, he chose to prove that he was *not* dependent for life on the beneficence of the great Nebuchadnezzar.

It's the issue that today's Christians have almost forgotten: does our life consist in the things which we have—materially and physically—of this world's good things? God's Word states emphatically that it doesn't—or shouldn't. Yet who could deny that many, perhaps most, of God's supposedly separated people are a merged and melted and scarcely recognizable Anyface in the cauldron of humanity?

Determined not to be defiled—but discreetly determined. That was Daniel. The careful screening that had placed him in this enviable position demanded young men who had the ability to stand in the king's presence. No slouches, these four. They were sharp and wise as serpents, as well as being good-looking and healthy specimens. And of course Daniel was the cleverest of them all. When none of the king's astrologers could recall and interpret for him his dream, Daniel's big chance came. First he had the moral authority to counsel the captain, sent to slay every last one of the unsuccessful astrologers, to calm down. Then he had the audacity to ask for an audience with Nebuchadnezzar himself to plead for time. *He* would reveal the king's dream himself. Whatever the revelation turned out to be, whether agreeable to the king or not, Daniel guaranteed to tell all.

How gratifying the interpretation turned out to be when it came. In the composite image that Daniel described, Nebuchadnezzar ruled supreme as the head of gold. Other kingdoms would rise and fall, but none would equal this "king of kings." What budding politician wouldn't love to tell his mentor such news. But wily Daniel was thinking all the time and when Nebuchadnezzar fell down and worshiped the wise interpreter, Daniel was already phrasing the request that would put his three friends into positions of influence in the realm. As for himself, he'd be sitting in the king's gates—of that he could be sure.

Not only was Daniel determined to *be* something for God, but he was also determined to *do* something significant in spite of the loneliness he undoubtedly faced as a stranger in a strange land. Samson had offered himself, at the tail end of his life, as a dead sacrifice. Daniel used his wits to offer himself far more significantly as a *living* sacrifice. Survival has definite merit when one is being useful for God, and, undeniably, the man with the divinely appointed political craft had set himself up for influence.

How he survived . . . year after lonely year . . . kingdom after kingdom. Courting the noose wasn't for him. "Don't these Christians have enough hemp to hang themselves?" complained a Roman prosecutor of the third century. Some Christians, indeed, were probably guilty of being overzealous for martyrdom. Daniel mixed discretion with courage—and survived to be God's continuing instrument in succeeding kingdoms.

Principled but amiable. That was the route Daniel took. The result was tremendous influence for good and for God, without his ever being influenced by men or circumstances. He was tough, durable, resilient—but never pliable or plastic. Never was there a more independent captive. A politician like Daniel every nation could use!

Understandably pleased to have rated top billing in Daniel's interpretation, Nebuchadnezzar ordered a monumental image of himself constructed on the Plain of Dura. All gold, from head to foot, it was designed by the fatuous king to receive the worship of his adoring subjects. The musical cacophony which preceded each obeisance didn't seem to inspire Shadrach, Meshach, and Abednego, however, and they remained unbowed. Faithful Daniel. His own determination had borne fruit. It could have been he speaking: ". . . be it known unto thee, O king, that we will *not* serve thy gods nor worship the golden image which thou hast set up."

But why not bend the knee? What did it signify anyway? One could remain true of heart—even while one performed the simple gesture. With similar logic some of the third-century Christians dropped the required pinch of incense on the pagan altars, and lived. Not the three young Israelites. They went the distance and took the consequence. When they came out of the fiery furnace unsinged, they must have smiled to hear the decree condemning to an even more horrible death all those who refused to bow down to their great God.

"I wisdom dwell with prudence . . ." (Proverbs 8:12) said Solomon. Without being in touch with God no human maneu-

vering could have led these four past the Scylla and Charybdis
of conscience's demands and Nebuchadnezzar's power. But the
tremendous moral victory they gained at their *first* confrontation with Babylon's choices set the stage for their whole future
in that land. There wasn't only the assurance in their own
hearts that a right moral choice had been made, but the ruler
of the kingdom of darkness had been served notice as to what
to expect in the future.

Not only is the world itself a vast Babylon, but we step daily
from our safe islands of security, whether home or church or
Christian circles of friendship, into any number of Babylonian
kingdoms. For most young people school is that first real confrontation with "the king's meat." How easy to slip through the
four or five years undetected as an alien. The language is Babylon's—the dress, tastes, the things that amuse, the affections.
". . . If any man love the world, the love of the Father is not
in him" (1 John 2:15). Daniel speaks to us across the ages.
Protect yourself. Refuse the king's meat the *first* time it's set in
front of you. Once eaten, it's easier to accept it again . . . and
easier . . . and easier. Once refused, it's easier . . . and easier
. . . to refuse again.

Precedent established, Daniel handled his second political
crisis with the aplomb of an expert. Imagine Kissinger's telling
Ford that unless he repents and shows mercy to the poor he'll
be afflicted with madness and be put out to pasture to eat grass!
Daniel not only said it to Babylon's king, but when the prophecy had come to pass and madness had run its course, Nebuchadnezzar returned in his right mind to the palace to extol
Daniel's God. It was a rare piece of influence peddling, if you
will. That Nebuchadnezzar fell for it was no doubt in large part
because he knew that a man who was willing to risk his head
on a thing like the food he ate wouldn't be afraid to lose it over
a piece of bad news like this. It *had* to be the truth.

Nebuchadnezzar's son ruled in his place—the arrogant Belshazzar. Daniel was still around, but forgotten—momentarily.

When Belshazzar, too, had a warning visitation from God, the memory of a certain fearless Israelite prophet surfaced and Daniel was summoned. Gifts, a chain of gold, the third position in the kingdom—it was his if he'd interpret the fearsome vision. No warning this time, no *ifs* or conditions. The kingdom was doomed. The sentence fell from Daniel's lips with all the convincing power of truth. And still Daniel walked out of the palace that night wearing the promised chain of gold and invested with the third place in all the kingdom. A spectacular *tour de force* by Babylon's master politician? No. Long ago, when he'd first arrived, he'd counted the odds on making a stand for God and found they were all in his favor. Belshazzar, who had opted to live without God, lost his kingdom and his life that night—but again Daniel survived.

With practiced ease Daniel slipped into his appointed place of influence in the conqueror's government. By this time we're not surprised that ". . . this Daniel was preferred above the presidents and princes, because an excellent spirit was in him; and the king thought to set him over the whole realm." Abrasive only when he needed to be, totally scrupulous, pleasing of disposition, he was bound to arouse frustrated jealousy. Was there no way to get rid of this interloper? Yes, there was. The wily plotters knew Daniel, as indeed everyone did by now, as incorruptible concerning the law of his God. If the king could be flattered into signing into law a decree forbidding the asking of a petition of anyone except the king himself for thirty days, they'd have him. Three times a day he prayed toward Jerusalem —with his windows open. It was no secret. He was as good as in the lions' den already.

Now we all know how hard it is to bow our heads and pray in a public restaurant in "Christian" America. Only fanatics are expected to do anything more than rub their eyes or fuss with their hair to cover the painful duty. Imagine, then, Daniel's flinging wide his window and lifting his devout eyes toward the Holy City in prayer. The third ruler in the land knew the decree as well as anyone. Calmly he prayed.

The story is familiar to everyone. The crime is discovered. The king could kick himself for having signed such a law, but he must honor his decree. In goes Daniel into the den of lions and away goes Darius to spend the night in sleepless fasting. The next morning he hurried exhausted to the lions' den to find a refreshed and cheerful Daniel. No damage, he assures the king. And again God makes the wrath of man to praise Him when the decree goes out that throughout the kingdom men should tremble and fear before the God of Daniel—or suffer the consequences.

Job speaks of a path which no fowl knows and which the vulture's eye has not seen. (See 28:7.) The path that Daniel trod would hardly be an obvious one. Most of us could imagine ourselves acting in any other way than he in similar circumstances. Is it any wonder, then, that so many of the so-called chosen ones of our day quickly melt from view among Babylon's populace? How much better to accept the divinely appointed solitariness which must come in those situations in which a choice must be made between the expedient and the right? The straight and narrow way is not a well-traveled road. Daniel came to Babylon a captive: he remained to become a ruler, but always on behalf of his real Master. Influential as he was, he wasn't around much unless he was needed. The social round of government circles wasn't for him; nor did he find it necessary for keeping his position. Certainly he wasn't at the dedication of Nebuchadnezzar's golden image. If he had been, there would have been a fifth figure in the fiery furnace. Nor was he at the high-level office party which was Belshazzar's feast. Human companionship wasn't so necessary to him that he would compromise to gain it.

What did Daniel really lose by that youthful determination to be a standout for God wherever he was? Nothing. He didn't even lose a night's sleep in the lions' den. Separation from the world only causes suffering if we think we're missing something worthwhile. The sense of values is the crucial point. In 1956 five young men chose to turn their backs on promising careers and certain worldly success to bring the Gospel to one of the most savage of Ecuador's tribes. Their death by Auca spears made news around the world. A waste of young life? Hardly. One of them had written in his diary years before, "He is no fool who gives what he cannot keep to gain what he cannot lose." Daniel survived, but only because he was prepared to die, to be expendable. He could have died, as Jim Elliot did, but God had appointed him to life.

Kings came and went and Daniel remained to receive from God the prophecies which would mark the end-times. "And I Daniel *alone* saw the vision," he declares in the third year of Cyrus. How typical. ". . . and there remained no strength in me. . . . Yet heard I the voice of his words. . . . And he said unto me, O Daniel, a man greatly beloved, understand the words that I speak unto thee, and stand upright: for unto thee am I now sent."

The man who stood alone and yet wasn't alone was the man with the mission. Amazing that he could last so long without the king's meat? Daniel's answer would have been the same as Christ's, ". . . I have meat to eat that ye know not of." That meat and the fellowship of the One who walks with His own in the furnace of life was Daniel's antidote to the loneliness he might otherwise have succumbed to as a stranger in a strange land.

12

"I Have No Man"

One of the most heartbreaking stories in all of the Bible is recorded in John 5. Bethesda of the five porches was the scene of a misery so vast that the name itself has been given to countless hospitals throughout the land. Near the sheep market with its raucous tumult of bleating animals and the strident voices of those who bought and sold, within earshot of all the sounds that go with the vigorous competitive human spirit, lay "a great multitude of impotent folk." Not for them the hope of turning a dollar by their wits. The fact that these wretches had perhaps been senators, captains of merchant ships, high priests of the temple, or any number of proud and important personages had been canceled out in their present misery.

The blind and halt and withered who lay there had only one thought in mind—a competition of sorts also—but one whose stakes were far higher than those involved in the shrewd deals being closed nearby or even the successful return of a treasure-laden merchant ship. Before all of these helpless human beings dangled a hope—a very small one indeed—but that one small possibility which alone makes life—and suffering—tolerable. *If* the blind or lame one had a friend nearby, and *if* that friend could help to lower him into the Pool *first* after the angel of the Lord had moved the water, then—glorious result—that one came out of the Pool whole and healed. It was one chance in perhaps a thousand, but it was a hope which kept each one of those desperate human beings from despair.

But there was one who had no such hope. Already he had spent more than his life's expectancy lying within sight of an elusive miracle that was always for others. How often he'd seen a loving son or father or friend hasten to lower one of his fellow sufferers into the Pool. He'd seen the look of compassion and the answering gratitude on the face of the one who clung to his benefactor as he was carried to the healing waters. How often he'd heard the cry of joy—as someone long blind beheld anew the blue of the sky or discovered the use of a withered limb or felt the inner healing that restored a forgotten zest for life. For thirty-eight years he'd observed with languid eyes the dawn of each new day with its promised miracle and had known for a certainty that the miracle would not touch him.

Thirty-eight years is a very long time, indeed, when it's spent in one place, seeing the same scene unfold every day, hearing the same conversations, invariably centering on the same subject.

"Today Philip is coming. I hope he gets here in time. Perhaps this will be *my* day. By the way, Simon, don't you have a friend?"

"No, I have no friend."

Or, "See I've gotten right to the edge. The angel moved the waters here last time. Perhaps if my son gets me down quickly enough, *I'll* be the one healed next. . . . Say, don't you have a family that cares about you?"

"No, no family. Nobody who cares."

Or perhaps: "I hear you've been here a long time. Surely during all these years *someone* has offered to help you!"

"No. No one. I have nobody."

And so it went. An incredible thirty-eight years went by, and countless times during each of those years he'd missed his chance for healing because he had no one who cared. Of course there were others who weren't healed—many others—but at least they had the hope that one day the moment would be right, and they'd walk away forever from this imprisoning place.

This day seemed no different from a thousand others until the moment when a shadow fell across the inert heap that was Simon. Who could be lingering by his side? Those who came on errands of mercy here always passed him by. They were always in a hurry—to go to someone else's side.

But now, very definitely, someone was stopping beside him, concentrating his attention on him alone. It was when Simon looked curiously up at the face of the tall figure who lingered still so strangely by his side that his world turned upside down. Far more than curiosity or casual interest could be read there. It was a look he'd seen often, but always it had been directed at someone else. Now those penetrating eyes that seemed to have the capacity to encompass all of human suffering were looking into his with compassion. Gone was all remembrance of his own suffering, of his bleak surroundings, even of the miracle that was never for him. Someone cared—he couldn't mistake the look—and his heart melted within him.

But in the next instant the moment was interrupted with the words, "Wilt thou be made whole?" The tenderness had been so beautiful. Now he was reminded of the whole miserable meaning of this wretched place—the sight and smell of illness, the discordant noise from the sheep market, and his generation-long sojourn here. But most of all he was reminded that he wasn't like other men. *He* had no friend, and precisely for that reason he'd never had a chance to be made whole. To be so long friendless had molded his total outlook on life.

There was a questioning look in those eyes. An answer was expected. And the answer was as strange as the question, in fact it was no answer. It was a cry out of hell—the hell in which every lonely and uncared-for human being lives.

"I have no man."

But—the question was, "Wilt thou be made whole?" Didn't you hear it, Simon?

Shall we dare to say that Simon *didn't* hear it, or if he did, that the problem of his illness was far less important to him than the fact that no one cared?

He plucks at Jesus' robe. "Listen . . . I have no loved one like these others, and now You, a total stranger, *You* stop to talk to *me*. I have no claim on You. I have nothing to give You. You care enough about me to single me out from all the rest. You care? Stay . . . stay a bit. What was it You were saying? Never mind. It doesn't matter. Just stay and talk to me a while. Let me hear the sound of Your voice again."

Whether the words were spoken or only inwardly felt, a change had begun taking place. Under that benevolent eye and hearing the sound of that gentle voice, something began rearranging itself in Simon's thinking. He was worth something after all. This kind Stranger's presence, even His silence, was like a benediction on his spirit. "Yes, Simon," he says to himself, "someone does care for you, and that's the most important thing in the world."

Into the deliciousness of this new experience comes the command, "Rise, take up thy bed and walk."

The order made no more sense than the question had, but they weren't words to comprehend but to experience. Into those withered legs surged the energy of divinely commanded strength. Simon got up and walked. It was that simple. To this helpless man Jesus gave no conditions as He had to the blind man at the Pool of Siloam or as Elisha had given to Naaman. Jesus didn't tax or even challenge his faith. The gift had been totally on the basis of his need.

The need? What had been the need? What is the need today? Why, salvation—of course. We need men and women of God who can drive the Gospel home with the ringing cry, "Wilt thou be made whole?" and then follow it up with the method: "Believe on the Lord Jesus Christ and thou shalt be saved." But

Simon hadn't answered the question—perhaps hadn't even heard it. The searing wound in his spirit which would not be healed was caused by an utter totality of alone-ness. That in itself was a crippling factor—emotionally if not physically. But he had met a Stranger who cared, and this Stranger had healed him with a word. What of the angel and the miraculous moving of the water? That was for others. That was for those who must wait for the faithful friend to lift the diseased or crippled burden into the tumult of the water. The healing would be for only one. For the rest there was the hope—perhaps next time.

Uncomprehending, Simon took up his bed and walked. And as he walked, he discovered that something else had happened as well. With the healing had come a new authority. In the face of the spiteful Jews who immediately pounced on him for carrying his bed on the Sabbath, he had a ready answer: "He that made me whole told me to take up my bed and walk." Already there was a change in his reactions to his fellowmen. Schooled in the perspective of thirty-eight forgotten years, he could now walk in the strength and authority of the One who had come to him where he lay.

Once more Jesus meets Simon, this time in the temple, surely an appropriate place for one who had so much to give thanks for. The account is sketchy, but the confrontation is plain—in the temple, the house of God, Simon comes to know the true identity of his benefactor.

True to His character, Jesus prepares Simon to face a world in which he is already a very real personage, in fact an object of contention. No longer is Simon a nonentity among the sick and dying. He's been restored—his wounded spirit made whole and his impotent body infused with energy—and the loving Stranger pursues him still, even to the temple.

Is the message clear? We Christians call ourselves servants of Jesus Christ. Do we serve in the way of Bethesda? How about the quality of our ministry to the lonely? Does it bear the marks of Christ's own compassion? The whole Creation groans and travails together. Imagine the poolside as a type of our world. It's a scene of total misery. Every one of those lying there is devastated not only by the ravages of sin, but by some personal catastrophe. They lie insulated and isolated in their own small universe of agony, rubbing elbows with hundreds of others in similar pain. And yet the universal groaning and travailing can be borne if, in the background, there is a friend, that *one* who is sufficient to keep hope alive.

Of course Christ is Saviour, but He is also the ultimate Friend —of the fatherless, the widow, the downcast, the sinner. And He has placed us here as His representatives, not only to preach the Gospel, but to minister to needs. The living waters are for life, but they are also for the refreshing of those who labor and are heavy laden. Christ tells us to bear one another's burdens. If it was not good for man to dwell alone in the Garden before the Fall, even less can he dwell alone in a world that is fragmented by the accumulation of several thousand years of sin and misery.

Let us assume, as devoted followers of our Master, that we truly do want to follow in the way of Bethesda. We know there are Simons at the office, next door, even—God forbid—in our church. Perhaps we have identified at one time with Simon ourselves and have experienced the healing that a very special friend has brought into a time of loneliness. What then was the secret of Jesus' ministry at the Pool of Bethesda?

First of all, Jesus was in the right place. There's a beautiful chorus that has no doubt been sung lustily by thousands upon thousands of Christians in Sunday schools, at campfires, youth retreats, on sofas, easy chairs, perhaps even in bed with a feather pillow under one's head. "Make Me a Blessing" has no doubt brought many a lump into good Christian throats. It's not likely Jesus sang it that day in Jerusalem, but He knew and acted upon its message ". . . make me a blessing to someone today." Because He meant it, He headed for the sheep market and beyond it to the Pool of Bethesda. It wasn't a pleasant

place, that sheep market, with the dust swirling up from tram-
pling feet and the smell and the noise. The Pool was even less
pleasant. It was a place of groans, emaciated bodies, running
sores, deformed limbs. Who would choose to go there unless
motivated by a very special love? Jesus came to *seek* and to
save. He *went* where the needy were.

Too often the words of the chorus become a meaningless
sentiment, "Lord, *make* me a blessing. Drop a golden opportunity square in my lap right where I'm sitting and I'll show You
what wonders I can do in Your name." No, go to the Bethesda
Pool and you won't have to beg to be made a blessing. Christ
calls us to involve ourselves, to *go* to those who are lonely and
needy. The first lesson then, if we are sincere, is to be in those
places and in those situations where we are most likely to
encounter needs.

The second requirement seems to involve a certain spiritual
discernment that goes beyond just being where the need is. If
the Pool is a small picture of our world, quite obviously every
human being is in some way impotent and needs the interven-
tion and interaction of other human beings. How many prone
bodies Jesus had to pass by to reach Simon's side we don't
know. We can be sure He looked with compassion on all of
them, but it was to this particular man He directed His steps.
It was Simon, who had nobody (nor indeed likely ever had had
anybody), that drew Jesus' attention. He needed someone to
care about him *personally,* one-to-one. It would have been easy
for Jesus to stand at one end of the portico and deliver a sermon.
Never did preacher have a more captive nor a more needy
audience. He could have done it "with His eyes closed"—
literally—and moved on with the virtuous feeling that the
golden opportunity of the day had not been missed. Or if He
wasn't the sermonizing type, He could have brought in a quar-
tette to sing rousing gospel songs. Or how about some scenic
slides, or a bit of entertainment from the local Christian drama
group, to put it in a more contemporary setting? It would pass

the time, distract the sufferers, do so much for so many.

But we're told that Jesus "saw *him* lie," and He stopped by this lonely and forgotten man's side. Others had seen him lie as well—many, many others. Possibly during those long years some had stopped to look, even as the Levite had looked at the one wounded by thieves and left to die by the roadside. But it takes a Good Samaritan's eye and heart to cause one to recognize that this is the one that's for *you* at this moment.

The heart of love just somehow gravitates toward the most hopeless and the most unlovely. "The quality of mercy is not strain'd," Shakespeare tells us. It deals with a generous hand and with a joyous spirit. It doesn't qualify its gift. Not satisfied with "mercy drops" as we often sing, it's "showers of blessing *we* plead." Then, conversely, we should be prepared to deal with a liberal hand. That liberality is the third beautiful quality of Christ's ministry to the lonely. "Lord, make me a blessing —a whole, sufficient according-to-the-need blessing." Not, "If I'm not too tired"; or, "Later"; or, "If I'm appreciated"; or a myriad of other easy-to-conjure-up qualifications. ". . . not as the world giveth, give I . . ." says our Divine Example. How do *we* give and with what attitude?

And finally, Jesus had the grace to give Simon no patronizing words of advice—at first. How contrary to human nature that is, like everything our Lord would have us do in His name. But wait. The Bible is full of good counsel. How about "He who would have friends must show himself friendly"? (*See* Proverbs 18:24.) "Surely, Simon, during all these years you've cultivated *some* sort of relationship with someone!"

"No—no one."

"Well, what kind of person are you? Look at all these others —they all have *somebody* to help."

"Yes, but I have no one."

"Now that's really too bad. You should develop some social know-how. Learn how to win friends and influence people. Make yourself available . . . socially attractive. . . ."

Of course we've gotten out of the Bethesda context and uncomfortably into the arena of our own lives. How quickly the pinpointing of blame comes, whether voiced or merely thought. And if only thought, how surely the patronizing tone creeps in and sinks like a dead weight into the already troubled heart. "Do you want to get in on the social scene, buddy? Well, let me give you some advice." Of course the implication is that there must be some change before this misfit can be accepted.

"Wilt thou be made whole?" The question stands alone. No platitudes or impossible prerequisites. There is no faith to be praised nor any lack of it for which to be upbraided. Poor Simon doesn't even know how very sick he is, even down to his heart's core. But he does know that he needs help, not advice. What, after all, *can* an impotent man do? And so his cry is, "I have no man." The desperate cry came from Simon's lips, but the sound is taken up by countless voices and echoed and reechoed throughout the far reaches of this groaning Creation. "I'm alone, stranger. That's all I know. About the other—the reason for it—I don't know. I need someone, one person—like these others, just one."

Jesus in His infinite wisdom knew that Simon's need—our need—was greater than that, but He accepted Simon's assessment because He knew that without that first step toward wholeness Simon could not take another. Can we be so gracious? Or even more to the point, can we be so sensitive that we recognize the true need when it's not voiced, even as Jesus did when talking to the woman at the well?

The impotent ones around us today need the same quality of love. "While we were yet sinners Christ died for the ungodly" (Romans 5:8). With gratitude we acknowledge that it had to be this way or not at all. "Not by works of righteousness which we have done, but according to his mercy he saved us . . ." (Titus 3:5). If our salvation was granted with such exquisite grace, then shouldn't those who have experienced that healing love be moved to love the same way in return? Simon didn't love the kind Stranger looking down at him so tenderly. He needed to *be* loved. In his ocean of loneliness he needed what Jesus had to give—the honest heart that had directed His footsteps to a place of need, the singling out of that particular one among so many, and the no-strings-attached love which "upbraideth not." Simon had absolutely nothing to offer, yet Jesus cared anyway. Like a magnet He was attracted to those in need—the miserable, the diseased, the outcast.

You and I are His followers. "Following Jesus, ever day by day . . . He leads the way." We've often sung it. And how do good Bible-believing, hardworking church members show that they are these faithful followers? By dispensing love and good works and precious time as a reward to the worthy—of course. Who of us could deny it? And through the murky ugliness of good deeds done as favors and love rationed according to merit and time given by timetable, echoes still the unsatisfied cry from beside the Pool, "I have no man. No one just to love me. No one to be sorry even though he *can't* help me. Alone—utterly alone."

Without advice or conditions, Jesus proved that He was indeed what He was accused of being—a friend of sinners. His whole nature expressed love. It was as natural as breathing. How very right to speak of the *gift* of love. It's not something dispensed in payment of a debt or in the form of a wage. It's a gift. One must receive it with open and *empty* hands.

Simon had been healed—in spirit and in body—and in a daze he picked up his bed and walked. Whether he thanked his kind benefactor or not, we don't know, but sure it is that we next find him in the temple. Certainly it was more than curiosity that took him there. It was an exciting place, a place of concourse, of barter, with the clink of coins, the shouts of vendors. It was also still the place of worship, perverted as it had become. Let's hope that Simon went there to give thanks. If he did, he had the right idea, for doesn't the Word tell us, "We love him, because he first loved us" (1 John 4:19)? Now that Simon has met his friend and has been healed, he too has something to offer. But not before.

And it isn't until he entered the place of offering and of thanksgiving that Jesus confronted him with His identity and his (Simon's) own responsibility. Friendless by the Pool, friendless still in the streets of Jerusalem, the time had come for direction and guidance—in a word—*advice.* He was bewildered and uncertain, not yet a strong spiritual dynamo. Again Jesus was in the right place at the right time. "You are whole, Simon. Watch it now. Beware. Sin can bring you back to the Pool and worse. Remember who it was who commanded you to rise. The same One tells you to walk, carefully, remembering the past, aware of the consequences of a misstep. Above all, Simon, remember that it is I, Jesus, who made you whole, and it is I who tell you to walk worthy of your calling."

With the words "Sin no more" ringing in his ears, Simon disappeared from sight. We would hope that he was occasionally drawn back to the troubled Pool to minister to some disease-ridden wretch—someone who, like him, had no one. We'd like to believe he did, but we're not told. What a testimony he'd have had. What a powerful motivation to comfort others with the same comfort wherewith he'd been comforted. *Now* the love can operate in a two-way relationship. "We love him because he first loved us." He could give only what he'd received.

"Woe is me," Paul said, "if I preach not the news of salvation." It was a message he could not still. But do we cry with equal fervor, "Woe is me if I *practice* not my religion"? Certainly to practice is as important as to preach. And what is the religion we are to practice? Of religions there are many, but the one which is described as pure and undefiled is that which moves us "to visit the fatherless and the widow" (James 1:27) —the ones who are uniquely alone.

Do you really want to follow in the way of Bethesda? Then go to the Pool. Be honest. *Go* there. Does it mean visiting the local home for the aged? Go. Does it mean sitting next to the tongue-tied, all-thumbs loner at the church social? By all means sit there. Does it mean visiting the local university campus and letting it be known that your home is open to lonely foreign students? Then do it.

Does the message of Bethesda mean that you are willing to take time for *one* deep need when you could minister more spectacularly, accompanied by the plaudits of your fellow Christians, to many? Then be as David's poured-out cup of water from the well of Bethlehem and offer your gift in this humble way.

Does it mean that you stifle your urge to dispense pearls of wisdom—even scripturally sound ones—in order to prove a love that's patient and "vaunteth not itself" (1 Corinthians 13:-4)? Then keep quiet, even as Jesus did, and get on with the work of healing through loving. Just as our heart's cry becomes "I love him because he first loved me," so the Simons in our lives learn the grace of loving because they themselves have learned the art from the one who loved them in their need.

Simon, where are you now? The encounter was so brief, but the healing so complete. Multiplied millions of today's Simons still lie at the Pool—waiting. Jesus stands in pity by their side, but they don't recognize Him. His real flesh and blood representatives are busy elsewhere—always elsewhere. Are we willing to take our place as the graciously healed Simons of this world and go back to the Pool?

"I have no man" is still too often the cry that answers Christ's beseeching question, "Wilt thou be made whole?" The Pool beckons. Go there.